EXILE ON MAIN ST.

THE ROLLING STONES

Other titles in Schirmer's *Classic Rock Albums* series

LET IT BE / ABBEY ROAD
THE BEATLES

Peter Doggett

NEVER MIND THE BOLLOCKS,
HERE'S THE SEX PISTOLS
THE SEX PISTOLS

Clinton Heylin

DISRAELI GEARS
CREAM

John Platt

THE RISE AND FALL OF ZIGGY STARDUST
AND THE SPIDERS FROM MARS
DAVID BOWIE

Mark Paytress

MEATY, BEATY, BIG AND BOUNCY
THE WHO

John Perry

NEVERMIND
NIRVANA

Jim Berkenstadt and Charles R. Cross

MURMUR
R.E.M.

John Platt

CLASSIC ROCK ALBUMS
Series Editor: Clinton Heylin

EXILE ON MAIN ST.

THE ROLLING STONES

John Perry

SCHIRMER BOOKS
An Imprint of Macmillan Library Reference USA
New York

Acknowledgments can be found on page 131, and should be considered an extension of the copyright page.

SCHIRMER BOOKS
An Imprint of Macmillan Library Reference USA
1633 Broadway
New York, NY 10019

Library of Congress Catalog Card Number: 99-31644

Printed in the United States of America

Printing number
10 9 8 7 6 5 4 3 2 1

Library of Congress Cataloging-in-Publication Data

Perry, John.
  The Rolling Stones, Exile on Main St. / John Perry.
      p.   cm. — (Classic rock albums)
  Includes bibliographical references and index.
  ISBN 0-02-865063-8
  1. Rolling Stones. Exile on Main St.   2. Rock music—History and criticism.
  I. Title.   II. Series.
ML421.R64P47   1999
782.42166'092'2—dc21   99-31644
                                                                          CIP

This paper meets the requirements of ANSI/NISO Z39.48-1992 (Permanence of Paper).

CONTENTS

THE REVIEWS   102

For Maria

ACKNOWLEDGMENTS

For their assistance and generosity, my thanks are due to Nina Antonia, Carlos Arias, Steve Brickle, Richard Carlin, Peter Ceresole, Clinton Heylin, Prince Rupert zu Loewenstein, Maria McCormack, Andrew Neill, Patti Palladin, Anita Pallenberg, Lord Parmoor, Bill Plummer, Carol Price, Suresh Raja, Stephanie Zacharek, and the staff of the British Newspaper Library at Colindale.

Finally, a special cheer for Peter Roe, who, many years ago on the morning of my twentieth birthday, turned up at my doorstep bearing "the new Stones album."

John Perry

INTRODUCTION

AS THEY SAY IN JAMAICA, IT IS
ROUGH TO BE DE KING, MON.

—Keith Richards

EXILE IS THE WOUND OF KINGSHIP.

—Anthony Powell

As Keith used to say, if you're going to get wasted, you might as well do it elegantly. Similarly, if you're going into voluntary exile, you may as well go in comfort—and by the spring of 1971, the Rolling Stones could afford considerable degrees of both comfort and elegance.

Those who come from the street know the street; those who don't must either learn its ways, hire good protection, or suffer the consequences. Main Street has its attractions, but the going is tough and the locals tend to bite. Better by far to view the street on your own terms. Take what you need and slip away silently into the night; a sleek vehicle with comfortable leather seats, darkened windows, and a fine mansion at journey's end.

Speaking to Robert Greenfield shortly before the release of *Exile on Main St.* in May 1972, Jagger located Main Street in downtown Los Angeles, describing a scene where "you can see pimps, knives flashin', real inner city," and in doing so, he also pinpointed the paradox that lay at the core of the Rolling Stones as they neared their tenth anniversary.

The white English rock band, who, better than any of their contemporaries, had distilled the essence of black American blues and fashioned from it a hybrid body of original work, were now powerful, wealthy men. The scruffy upstarts who had inevitably been cast as the villainous counterparts to the cheerful, smiling Beatles may still have been cultivating the odd nasty habit, but insulated by money, influence, and the finest merchant bankers in Europe, they were about as far as it's possible to get from the vagabond life typified by their blues heroes.

The band that arrived in L.A. that summer was there to begin a two-month tour of North America promoting a new double album, recorded on its own studio equipment and released on its own record label. In 1972, the Rolling Stones were the number one act in show business, bar none: the hottest ticket in town. So far as the Ticketron outlets who sold the seats were concerned, it was Exile on Mainstream.

The previous U.S. tour, in 1969, had pushed the old ways, the original Rolling Stones creed to its limit—tested it to destruction in fact, and a very nasty mess it had made too, when the pieces had finally come flying off in all directions, at a speedway in the scrubby hills beyond Livermore, outside San Francisco. The band had taken brinkmanship to the very edge of the abyss, so let nobody point the finger when they decided to Get Organized.

By 1972 the Rolling Stones were a very long way indeed from any conventional notion of "street"; further, in fact, than the average fan of the day had any real way of comprehending. They looked in great shape—cooler than ever—yet they had recently been closer than anyone supposed to Queer Street, an old English term denoting bad circumstance, penury, terminal debt, bankruptcy, and ruin.

The album *Exile on Main St.* is thus a triumph on at least two levels. As well as being a musical tour de force, it represents the victory of a band over some of the most powerful commercial forces at work in the late-1960s music world; forces that had proved too much for the weakened Beatles to withstand and that might just as easily have engulfed the Stones, who had their own problems in the form of the fading Brian Jones.

Instead of fading away, however, leaving *Beggar's Banquet* or *Let It Bleed* as their epitaph, the Stones regrouped, found a replacement guitarist, and a merchant banker to guide them from the edge of bankruptcy, set up their own label, and went on to record the finest double album of blues-based rock 'n' roll in existence.

Ladies and Gentlemen, *Exile on Main St.*

The Rolling Stones introduce
their new lineup at a press
call in Hyde Park, June 13,
1969. Left to right: Charlie
Watts, Mick Taylor, Mick
Jagger, Keith Richards,
Bill Wyman.
(Photo: Corbis/Bettmann)

THE STORY

Exile on Main St. was issued in the summer of 1972, the Stones' second album release on their own record label. Recorded in the south of France and completed in Los Angeles, it crowns the sequence of classic LPs that appeared between 1968 and 1972—*Beggar's Banquet, Let It Bleed* (both on Decca Records), *Sticky Fingers,* and *Exile on Main St.* (Rolling Stones Records)—all produced by Jimmy Miller.

Miller subsequently produced one more Stones album, *Exile on Main St.*'s successor, the watery *Goat's Head Soup* (recorded in Jamaica, 1973), but something went astray with the process. The record has an odd, slightly out of kilter feel. Tracks that ought to work never quite settle. Keith's attention seems to wander in and out of focus, and Jagger's rare sense of balance in the delicate art of self-parody had utterly deserted him.

Jimmy Miller told Nina Antonia:

> There was just this feeling through *Goat's Head Soup* that the whole thing was falling to pieces. Mick and Keith's relationship had started to go astray. I think Mick's marriage to Bianca had a lot to do with that because Anita and Bianca didn't get along. It was no longer Mick and Keith's song—it was Mick's song or Keith's song. I knew as we were doing it that it wasn't going to be a wonderful album.

By this time, Mr. Jimmy had his own problems too, but there's no doubting the accuracy of his assessment. After more than two decades' worth of subsequent albums, the "Jimmy Miller era" still stands as the

1

mature voice of the Stones. Those who've followed the band's entire career generally regard these albums as the Stones' most fertile period, with *Exile* itself as the definitive album, and indeed the last word, on the whole era.

Much of *Exile* can be read as a summary of, and an epitaph for, the 1960s. The songs are not all of a piece—many dating back three or four years to the Stones' heyday as late 1960s icons—more a loose collection of tracks, yet the continuity is unaffected. In fact the oldest track of all, "Shine a Light," is one of the strongest and most reflective pieces on the entire record.

Not that this is any sense a "concept album." There are few things grimmer than deliberate attempts to issue bulletins on The State of Rock—although we were never in much danger of that from the Stones. Like Dylan, they were far too self-possessed to fall into such gaucherie. Yet you don't rise from obscure blues clubs to the Top Twenty in less than twelve months, then spend the rest of one of this century's more turbulent decades at the epicenter of hip society without noticing the odd event around you.

From very early on in their package-touring days, the front-line members of the band became intrigued by the degree of control they exerted over their audiences. Well before Jagger had assembled anything like a coherent stage persona, Brian Jones could be seen quite deliberately baiting audiences with his tambourine—waving it in someone's face, challenging them to react. The front line were all interested in power, and throughout the decade the prevailing atmosphere within the inner circle—and around the whole band—seems to have been one of *tension.* It's a word used by almost every newcomer who managed to enter the circle.

With success, the Rolling Stones grew increasingly self-contained, and for a long time their instinctive reaction to anything new or unknown was a sneer. In itself, that's not so unusual among bands, but it's usually a collective defense against the outside world. The Stones were equally ready to sneer at each other, and the degree of ostracism directed at various members exceeded the normal dynamics of band interaction.

The front line were tough boys playing for high stakes, egged on by a bright manager with a taste for conflict. Amid a shifting pattern of alliances any display of weakness was likely to start a feeding frenzy.

Ruthless as they were with each other, their relations with the rest of the world were coldly functional. A pattern quickly developed whereby a useful outsider—an engineer, a photographer—would be adopted, brought inside the circle, employed, then dropped as soon as they were considered redundant. There would be no goodbyes, formal dismissals, or thanks for services rendered; one day the phone would just stop ringing and calls to the Stones' office would go unreturned. If any attempt was made to presume on existing acquaintance, a chance meeting at a club for instance, the unfortunate individual would simply be blanked.

The Stones developed a reputation for using people up. The pattern was still repeating itself after two decades, and the list of casualties is long. Michael Cooper, Jimmy Miller, Bobby Keys, Gram Parsons, Andrew Oldham, Brian Jones, Andy Johns—all either died or else drank and drugged themselves past the point where they were fit for consideration. Of the latter group, some recovered, some didn't. Either way, a band as busy as the Stones could afford no distractions.

A lot of fun was had, too. Youth, success, looks, money, social status are more than enough to make a person assume they're immune from the normal dangers of life. In Anita Pallenberg's words, "We thought we were the Kings of the Castle. Nobody could touch us." In those individuals where authentic devil-may-care natures were also present—and where every act merely enhanced that reputation—it's hardly surprising that the principals gradually felt their immunity extended through unrestrained hedonism and into class A narcotics.

While the *Sticky Fingers* album was being written and recorded (1969–70), such tokens of euphoria were still being waved about like trophies. *Exile on Main St.* takes a long step back from such posturing and casts a cold eye over the celebrations, and their cost. It makes no apologies and sets out no explanations, but it does offer a long, cool, unsentimental assessment of the state of play, at the end of a decade that promised so much.

Exile has a strong claim as the first rock album to make a full *tour d'horizon,* once the dust and debris of the 1960s had settled. With their base appetites satiated beyond measure (that game had grown too easy years before, by the time of songs like "Under My Thumb" and "Stupid Girl"), and with the band's founding member and several close friends dead, Mick and Keith were sufficiently intelligent to spot a new source of subject matter and articulate enough to set it down straight.

As the only major band still surviving from the earliest days, the Stones were uniquely placed to examine the decade they'd shaped and been shaped by. The Beatles had torn themselves apart, and the Who and the Kinks, though flourishing in different degrees, both came from a slightly later period of the 1960s. The one band who formed an unbroken link between the heyday of popstar package tours (1963–65) through the countercultural changes of 1966–68, into the post-1969 world of FM radio and "serious" LPs, was the Rolling Stones.

Way below them, the three-year cycle of the pop singles charts proceeded as ever. It's latest novelty was glitter-pop—mostly a collection of aged rockers from the (pre-Stones) Hamburg club days of 1961, squeezed into unbecoming costumes and somehow passed off on a new generation of prepubescent girls as the Latest Thing (though many of the revived artists were older than the Stones).

The real action was happening with albums, and since Dylan's abdication the crown belonged to the Stones by default. It was clear that they'd not only adapted to the changes, they were now leading them. *Exile* signaled a return to the black American music from which the band had grown—and from which they now fashioned an entirely contemporary album. With the passage of time, the scale of that achievement becomes clearer.

Background History

This is the story of a journey, a ten-year marathon that took a bunch of suburban English boys with a love of Chuck Berry and the blues, and a taste for pop-stardom, from the back rooms of London pubs to the French Riviera—a traditional playground for the international rich.

Even by the standards of the day, the Stones moved into the big league of British pop with almost indecent speed, going from their first regular club booking to the top of the bill on national package tours—the highest known level of success—in 11 months.

On Sunday nights, the Station Hotel in Richmond-on-Thames—one of the more pleasant, leafy, suburbs southwest of London—played host to the Crawdaddy Club, run by an energetic White Russian émigré named Giorgio Gomelski. After a series of one-off gigs, the Stones took over the Crawdaddy residency early in 1963, a job they held until they were booked onto their first national package tour in October 1963.

Gomelski had a word-of-mouth agreement to represent and promote the Stones, but his great interest was the new scene that was growing in his club, fueled by students from the nearby Kingston College of Technology. He decided to make a short film of the Stones and the excited crowd, which he hoped might be shown on television. Moved more by ideas than by money, Giorgio was essentially an enthusiast, and when it came to the hard edge of business he was easily sidelined by Andrew Oldham.

By April 1963 the buzz about the new band at the Crawdaddy was spreading around town. The Beatles came to see them. While Giorgio was away at his father's funeral in Switzerland, a fast-talking, 19-year-old hustler named Andrew Loog Oldham came down one Sunday night and chatted to Jagger and Jones during the interval. Oldham knew he had a winner, but he also knew he couldn't cope on his own.

He didn't waste time. Turned down by Brian Epstein—whom he offered a 50 percent stake in the group in exchange for financial assistance, facilities, and premises—and knowing that Gomelski would soon be back, he returned to the Crawdaddy the following Sunday with the man from whom he rented an office, an established agent/manager named Eric Easton.

Events accelerated with startling speed. The whole sequence from Oldham's first arrival to the signing of a Decca recording contract was achieved in less than a month. Oldham and Easton set up a company named Impact Sound, and on May 5, bandleader Brian Jones signed a three-year contract on behalf of the group. The jazz singer, author, and social commentator George Melly catches the essence in his book *Revolt into Style*:

> Without Jagger, without the Stones, it's possible that Rhythm and Blues might have remained a minority interest. [Jagger] was the charismatic Moses, waiting to lead R and B out of the clubs and into the promised land. The queues grew longer outside the Richmond Hotel. . . . On Sunday, 28 April 1963 . . . two gentlemen visited the premises. They were Eric Easton, a traditional pop-cum-showbiz-agent and his protégé Andrew Loog Oldham. Easton had reservations . . . Oldham had no reservations. Here were his ready made homunculi. He looked at Jagger as Sylvester looks at Tweetie Pie.

So who was this teenage whiz-kid Andrew Oldham—and where did he dream up a name like Loog?

Andrew was the illegitimate offspring of an English mother named Oldham and a Dutch-American named Loog, who was serving in England with the U.S. Air Force during World War II and was killed in action over Germany during 1944. The boy took both surnames: Andrew Loog Oldham. Like the Who's manager Kit Lambert, Oldham learned at school that in English life, authority—or its appearance—was everything. The class system ran so deep that the majority of Englishmen responded automatically to a certain diction and tone: the public-school educated, upper-class officer voice. With the correct tone, even a teenager could make headwaiters crawl. With sufficient nerve, and the correct bearing and attitude, you could get away with anything. Professional con artists had known this for centuries. In the 1960s a flamboyant group of young managers put it to use in the service of rock 'n' roll. The most notable beneficiaries were ourselves—we got the Stones and the Who.

Loog Oldham was educated at a small private preparatory school whose headmaster, so the boys believed, was often absent on vital spying missions for the Secret Service. The man was in fact a paroled prisoner, an ex–army officer who specialized in a particular form of the Long Firm scam: setting up private schools, taking fees, establishing good credit, then running up bills and retreating by moonlight just ahead of his creditors, to repeat the exercise in another part of the country. Such a valuable education wasn't wasted on the boy. In Philip Norman's phrase, it was "an early object lesson in the relation of fantasy to profit."

Leaving his public school, Wellingborough College, at age 16, Oldham blagged himself a job with Mary Quant, walking straight in off the street. Attracted by the glamour of pop, and encouraged by the fact that musical ability was unnecessary, he attempted, under a series of unlikely stage names, to become a singer. However, neither Sandy Beach nor Chancery Lane have left any profound impression on the pop world.

Here the story gets murky. Oldham, who already knew the value of inflating a story, talks of plans to kidnap an heiress, marry her, and sell the story to the papers (thereby creating three sources of income from a single act), but he soon found more legitimate employment as a PR assistant in the slack, pre-Beatles era music biz. In America these were doldrum years too (approximately 1960–63), when every other lightweight pop singer appears to have been named Bobby: Vee, Goldsboro, Comstock, Vinton, Darin, Rydell, and so on.

Working for a variety of clients, including Brian Epstein and the much-feared Don Arden, he eventually accepted an assignment that was to influence his life profoundly. The client was Phil Spector. Oldham copied every move Spector made. Though Oldham must have come across strong-arm tactics while working for Arden, Spector's youth, success, and gangster style made a lasting impression on him: the shades at midnight, the black-windowed limos, and 200-pound gun-toting "secretaries," the whole schtick that Spector had perfected in the course of becoming the Tycoon of Teen.

———

Over at Decca Records, Dick Rowe, the Man Who'd Turned Down the Beatles, was in a terrible state. When George Harrison tipped him off about the new band at the Crawdaddy, Rowe, desperate to remedy his Great Mistake, ran all the way to Richmond. He came, he saw, and he couldn't find anyone to talk to. He wanted the band all right, he wanted them desperately, but A&R (Artists and Repertoire) men had standards—they *never* spoke directly to musicians.

On Monday morning he tried, and failed, to find out who represented the Stones. Calling around all the usual agencies, he turned up nothing. Eventually he made contact with Eric Easton, and on May 14 Impact Sound signed a two-year deal to release *their* recordings of the Rolling Stones on Decca Records. Oldham had remembered Phil Spector's advice about recording in independent studios, thereby retaining the copyright.

A first single, Chuck Berry's "Come On," was released in June. The band said goodbye to the Crawdaddy in late September, when Eric Easton booked them onto their first package tour, a thirty-two-date swing through the Gaumont and Odeon cinemas of England, Scotland, and Wales, supporting the Everly Brothers and Bo Diddley.

Their second single, the Lennon/McCartney song "I Wanna Be Your Man," came out in November. Charting at number 12, it did well enough to put the Stones top of the bill on their second package tour, which started in January, just two months after the end of the first.

Between the two tours the Stones gigged almost nightly, playing the traditional circuit of ballrooms, clubs, town halls, and Corn Exchanges—including a date at the Cavern in Liverpool—and two London dates, either side of Christmas where they were supported by the Who. A third single—"Not Fade Away"—and a first LP were released, and by the end of May

1964 they'd completed their fourth U.K. package tour. In early June they set off for the United States.

In America the band worked small towns and state fairs, stopping to record in Chicago and Los Angeles. Of all the English bands, they were the quickest to learn that American studios had the facilities and the engineers to record rock music properly. What started off in Chicago as a pilgrimage to the spiritual home of Muddy Waters and Howlin' Wolf—Chess Records at 2120 South Michigan—quickly became a sound commercial exercise, as they emerged with recordings that had a depth and a polish unobtainable in England. Pressed up into seven-inch singles they made a sound that no other English band could produce.

The song that became their fourth U.K. single—a radical reworking of the Valentinos' "It's All Over Now"—was recorded in Chicago, where Chess engineer Ron Malo showed just what could be done if you weren't afraid to let the VU meters go into the red. He recorded the bass guitar deeper and fuller, tightened up the drum sound, and brought a new clarity to the top-line instruments, which threw Brian and Keith's twin guitar parts into stark relief—not so much lead and rhythm as left and right hands of a single guitar. On the chorus and the outro, the jangly, high treble flat-picking is highlighted against dark, heavily reverbed chords—a small masterpiece of engineering and arranging. On top, Jagger's vocal can hardly help but assume a new authority, as he turns the gospel pleading of Bobby Womack's original into the first of many carefully detailed condemnations of inconstant women.

From June 1964 until August 1966, the Stones used every American tour as a studio opportunity, recording albums and—more important in these years—all their singles in the U.S. Through 1965 their romance with America continued, Keith particularly, assimilating the influences that would eventually find their clearest expression on *Exile on Main St.*

At RCA Studios in Hollywood they recorded "The Last Time,"the first original Jagger/Richards composition to be issued as a single, working with a new sound engineer, Dave Hassinger. All the self-penned singles that define the Mark-1 Stones—"The Last Time," "Satisfaction," "Get Off of My Cloud," "19th Nervous Breakdown," "Paint It, Black," "Have You Seen Your Mother Baby, Standing in the Shadows?" and most of "Let's Spend the Night Together"—were recorded by Hassinger, under the nominal production of Andrew Oldham, with frequent contributions from arranger and keyboard player Jack Nitzche, Phil Spector's right-hand man.

It only takes a moment, looking at that list of singles, to see how quickly the breakthrough came. The finishing touches to "The Last Time" were added in February 1965. Three months later the same team was putting together one of the defining singles of summer 1965. A single that reached number 1 on both sides of the Atlantic, and broke America wide open for the Rolling Stones, was "Satisfaction."

From here on it was big time all the way—major shows, network television appearances, and more hits; a whirl of venues and faces. In the six months following the U.S. release of "Satisfaction," the Stones played 140 shows in America, Scotland, Norway, Finland, Denmark, Sweden, England, Ireland, Germany, Austria, then England and Wales again, before returning to Canada and the United States.

The Rolling Stones, on their first tour of America in 1964, meet costars Big Bertha and Tiny Tim, for their June 3 appearance on the Hollywood Palace television show. Left to right (standing) Mick Jagger, Keith Richards, Charlie Watts; (seated) Bill Wyman, Brian Jones. (Photo: Corbis/ Bettmann)

A well-organized financial engine was required to capitalize upon all this success. Even the experienced Eric Easton was out of his depth. In 1964 a man named Klein had approached Brian Epstein, offering to take over the Beatles' finances for him. Not unnaturally, Epstein politely declined this kind offer, but Klein began to take an interest in the "British Invasion." He got alongside Mickie Most, a London-based South African singer who'd moved into management, and started working with his artists. He got his hands on the Animals, the Dave Clark Five, Herman's Hermits, and the majority of Mickie Most's roster. He parted Donovan from both his managers and his record label, Pye Records, in a single weekend. "Did I steal him from Pye?" Klein asked rhetorically. "I stole him from Pye."

Allen Klein was a New Jersey–born hustler, raised in an orphanage after his mother's early death. An extremely hard worker with an exceptionally fast mathematical brain, badly dressed, and unprepossessing, he knew exactly how to make his apparent shortcomings work to his own best advantage—a Man for All Angles. His motto was, "There's no corporation in the world that doesn't have something to hide."

Putting himself through a night-school accountancy course, Klein first made his name auditing record company books on behalf of artists, finding unpaid royalties and monies supposedly "lost" in the pipeline. The record companies, deeply traumatized by the experience of actually paying out money to—of all people—their own artists, *hated* Klein. His audits usually discovered miraculous sums of money that the companies claimed must have been overlooked due to "accountancy errors" or "mislaid books."

In fact, Klein appears single-handedly to have identified a mysterious, almost biblical series of catastrophes that afflicted the American recording industry during the 1950s. Though many of the executives would undoubtedly have sacrificed their firstborn for a larger market share, they seem, by and large, to have escaped personal affliction (plagues of blains and boils, rains of frogs—that sort of thing). Their companies, however, suffered grievously. While the majority of departments functioned perfectly smoothly, right across the entire industry, in almost every company, the Accounts Payable departments were afflicted by the most rotten luck. When it came to paying the artist, it was always the same story. The ledgers had perished in floods or in fires, hurricanes and tornados—perhaps even in plagues of locusts.

Klein figured this was a bit fishy. Short, pudgy, not much to look at, he nonetheless struck the fear of God into the major corporations as one by one he audited their books and recovered sums of money as large as $100,000 for the artists he represented, including Eydie Gorme, Bobby Darin, and Bobby Vinton.

On the back of this growing reputation, in 1964 he was able to negotiate an advance from RCA records that actually reflected the true worth of America's premier soul singer/songwriter, the great Sam Cooke. Pop singer/songwriters were pretty rare in 1964, but not as rare as advances of $1 million. Cooke was shot dead not long after, in circumstances that have still never been satisfactorily explained.

A litigious man with a pronounced taste for firing off writs, Klein was an excellent fellow to have on your side when renegotiating an existing contract. One of Anita Pallenberg's home movies contains a scene shot from a car pulling up at Klein's residence. As the car comes to a halt on the gravel, a stout man in a pullover, hair greased back in a cowlick, descends a flight of steps to greet his visitors, sporting a big grin and a 12-bore shotgun.

Klein first became involved with the Stones' business affairs in 1965, invited in by Andrew Oldham, who needed assistance with the band's growing American affairs (and who also fancied the Rolls Royce that Klein promised him, "just like the one John Lennon owns"). The deal was that Klein would be Oldham's business manager and that Eric Easton—now surplus to requirements—would be ditched.

Klein set out to prove himself before any contracts with him were signed. Fortuitously for Klein, Impact Sound's original two-year deal with Decca was up for renegotiation. The story goes that Klein marched into the office of Decca boss Sir Edward Lewis and sprawled in a chair while all five Stones, wearing shades, stood in a silent semicircle behind him.

In his autobiography *Stone Alone,* Bill Wyman notes his own doubts about the deal, especially the speed with which it was being pushed through. He writes that Brian Jones began to share his doubts, while Keith Richards emerged as hawkishly pro-Klein. When Wyman suggested that they should at least be accompanied to the meeting by an independent lawyer, Keith told him, "Don't be so fucking mercenary. We've got to trust *someone.*" (A profoundly cynical observer might wonder if, even at this early stage, the songwriting team and major earners, Jagger/Richards, weren't party to more information than the other Stones.)

Sir Edward Lewis, an old-school English gentleman (who had been expecting a civilized chat with Eric Easton), was mauled in an assault that moved with bewildering speed between a machine-gun hail of figures and percentages and the language of the New Jersey back alleys. On the verge of shock, Sir Edward found himself agreeing to advance $1.25 million.

While all this was happening, it also emerged that Impact Sound (Oldham and Easton) had been receiving a 14-percent royalty from Decca since the initial signing in 1963, but had only been paying the band 6 percent. In addition, they were deducting their 25 percent management commission *from* the band's 6 percent. Somehow this was glossed over and presented as the sort of wrong that Klein would alleviate.

Under the new deal, the money would be paid out by U.S. Decca to avoid English tax problems and funneled through a complicated system

of companies into the Stones' company, Nanker Phelge. On August 28, 1965, the Stones and Andrew Oldham signed an agreement and an array of letters (reproduced at the back of Bill Wyman's book) that appointed Klein as comanager with Oldham. Michael Philip Jagger replaced Eric Easton as Chairman, and Charlie Watts became Company Secretary of Rolling Stones, Ltd.

The London newspapers announced that the Stones had a new manager. This was the beginning of a saga, which continues to this day, whose most notable detail is that the rights to all the Stones' 1960s recordings, including the majority of their most famous singles, are controlled not by the Stones but by Allen Klein. Even the release of *Exile on Main St.* was delayed when Klein claimed ownership to the copyright of several songs on the album. Jagger told *Melody Maker,* "The album should've been out by now [May 20, 1972]. It's down to Allen Klein. He claimed he had two tracks on it. We said we were gonna pay him, but it wasn't enough." Settlement has now been reached.

———

Around the same time that Klein turned up, another influential figure in the Stones story appeared, backstage at a show in Munich. Anita Pallenberg had grown up in Rome, where her family had long been connected with the arts, especially painting. As a teenager she'd hung out with Federico Fellini at Cinecitta, drifted into modeling and from there into films. A stunningly attractive blonde whose face shone in front of the camera, a career as a film star seemed hers for the asking. However, there was something more to Anita. Multilingual, bright, well educated, and naturally curious, she found modeling a bore. She wanted fun and was perfectly willing to stir things up if the results seemed likely to be amusing.

Anita spent the night with Brian Jones (who was already becoming deeply disturbed by the pressures inside the band), and pretty soon the two were living together in London. Anita continued to accept occasional acting jobs, but as she says, "I thought, why work so hard to be a film star when you could get the same treatment just hanging out with the Stones?"

The Jagger/Richards songwriting team had found its feet, and the Stones' singles were now all self-penned. Andrew Oldham favored the "Lock 'em in and churn 'em out" technique for writers and songs. This method worked well for Jagger/Richards but failed to answer for poor Brian Jones.

Bill Wyman on the 1972 tour.
(PHOTO: CORBIS/
LYNN GOLDSMITH)

Encouraged by Anita, Brian attempted to write songs, but always seemed to run into difficulties, resulting from two interlinked problems. The first was insecurity, a basic lack of confidence that remained masked for many years by his aggression and glamourous exterior; the second was a problem that afflicts many "natural" musicians. Brian could pick up almost any instrument and master it sufficiently to take into the studio, where his exotic instrumentation added color and texture to the Stones' recordings. He taught Jagger to play blues-harp and, as he tired of guitar, experimented with sitar, dulcimer, recorder, marimbas, glockenspiel, saxophones, mellotron—anything that came to hand. But as many have found, the roles of the natural musician and the songwriter are quite different—in fact a lack of technical knowledge is generally a benefit to the writer of pop songs. The natural player knows what chord *should* come next, and his critical faculties are always one jump ahead of his writing skills.

Since the power inside the Stones has always rested with Keith, the mid-1960s saw a seesawing of loyalties as Brian and Keith ganged up on Mick, then Mick and Keith formed an alliance against Brian; whoever had Keith's ear had control. But it was the string of original compositions that cemented the Jagger/Richards power axis, wrested the leadership of the band away from Brian, and eventually led to his dismissal, or retirement—interpret it as you will.

In the very early days, at the run-down Chelsea flat in Edith Grove, it had been Brian's energy, recklessness, and unshakeable self-belief that got the Stones on the road. While Jagger still wavered, trying to play it safe by continuing his daytime studies at the London School of Economics, Keith, the youngster of the group, lay around picking guitar and sleeping. It was the wild Welsh Jones, the undisputed bandleader—already the father of two illegitimate children—whose absolute conviction in the Stones and the future of R&B carried all before it. But a leader who neither composed nor occupied the frontman-vocalist position was *bound,* sooner or later, to run headlong into a power struggle, especially with two personalities as dominant as Mick Jagger and Keith Richards, and there was only one possible outcome.

Oldham always said that he encouraged the group to write its own material because it was the only guarantee of longevity in the post-Beatles pop world. This was true enough (although the Stones' first five singles [1963–65] were all covers), but Oldham was far too shrewd to overlook

Brian Jones outside the Court of Appeals, December 12, 1967. A nine-month prison sentence for drug possession was reduced to a £1000 fine. (PHOTO: CORBIS/HULTON-DEUTSCH COLLECTION)

the fact that songwriting was where real the money lay, and he wasn't shy about admitting it.

He'd learned too that the B side of a single generates the same amount of publishing income as the smash hit (or flop) on the A side. This info was probably gleaned from Phil Spector, who managed to get his own name on the B side of the first Stones session he attended—"Not Fade Away"/"Little by Little"—which took place soon after the U.K. tour on which the Ronettes appeared with the Stones. Spector was known to keep a jealous eye on his wife Ronnie, with good reason in this instance.

Oldham committed this knowledge to vinyl with the Andrew Loog Oldham Orchestra, in a dreadful pun on the old Music Hall standard and perennial coach-party singalong, "Oh I Do Like to Be beside the Seaside," which turns up as an Oldham/Watts/Wyman "original," "Oh, I Do Like to See Me on the B-Side."

———

By mid-decade several young entrepreneurs were looking for ways around the monopoly over the British recording scene held by EMI and Decca records. The two giant companies signed the artists, pressed the vinyl, distributed the product, and even sold the machinery on which records were played.

Well ahead of the pack were Andrew Oldham and Tony Calder, who formed Immediate Records in 1965 and lucked into a number 1 hit with their first signing—the U.K. rights to "Hang On Sloopy" by the McCoys. They also issued a single by Nico that predated her discovery by Andy Warhol for the Velvet Underground. They hit their stride with some classic records by ex-Ikette P. P. Arnold and by the Small Faces. The label also allowed Keith and Mick to serve as in-house writers and producers, giving them the chance to experiment with brass sections and orchestras, and re-record their own songs as singles for other artists.

Other indies followed, which in a scene as small as London involved much overlapping of talent and personnel. Shel Talmy, who produced three great early Who singles and also produced for Immediate, started the Planet label and issued records by the Creation. Robert Stigwood formed the Reaction label, which had Cream and, for a year, the Who. Then Kit Lambert and Chris Stamp formed Track records for the Who—and immediately landed Jimi Hendrix.

For some years a young Anglo-Jamaican named Chris Blackwell had been importing Jamaican music and licensing American blues records for his Island label. In the United States, drummer/producer Jimmy Miller was recording black bands from New York and New Jersey. Blackwell heard one of Miller's earliest productions, a George Clinton single, and liked it enough to bring Miller over to England.

Blackwell had a genuine love of music, and the Island Records ethos was simple. At its core lay two ideas—pick the best, and then trust them. Blackwell began assembling a family of talented individuals and gave them the time and the space to produce great music.

His first long-term signing was the teenage Steve Winwood. The early Spencer Davis Group hits "Keep On Running" and "Somebody Help Me" were built around the extraordinary ability of the 17-year-old Birmingham boy to sing like Ray Charles. He also played great Hammond Organ and doubled nonchalantly on lead guitar. Many consider that, had he chosen guitar as his main instrument, Eric Clapton's reputation as "God" may have been less secure, leaving him stranded as a common or garden archangel.

In a detailed interview for *Record Collector,* Jimmy Miller told Nina Antonia, "Chris Blackwell thought it might work for me to come over and do something with Steve and the Spencer Davis Group on 'Gimme Some Lovin'.' It changed my life, and it was their first hit in America."

It changed the Spencer Davis Group, too. Their early hits were catchy pop/R&B arrangements built around a fuzz guitar that owed more than a little to "Satisfaction"; the two Miller productions, "Gimme Some Lovin'" and its follow-up "I'm a Man," lifted the band onto a different level. Extremely intense, soulful records, they sounded like Ray Charles singing with complete abandon over a tight English hard-rock ensemble. The two records attracted a lot of attention. When Steve Winwood, following the mood of 1967, formed his own band Traffic, Miller went with him as producer.

Jimmy Miller recalled:

I was in Studio B in Olympic [Studios] and the Stones were in Studio A. We met in the kitchens. Traffic and I had just finished a really smoking track. Mick and Keith walked in as we were having a very loud playback, and the vibe was extremely positive. We visited their [*Satanic Majesties*] session later and nothing was happening; they were just sitting round. Mick told me how much he liked what I'd done with Spencer Davis and Traffic.

Back in Studio A something *was* happening, it just wasn't happening on tape. Mick and Keith found themselves increasingly out of sympathy with the man who'd done so much to position them in the pop world, and Andrew Loog Oldham found himself on the receiving end of the type of freeze-out he'd taught the boys in the first place. Photographer Gerard Mankowitz said, "We'd get to Olympic Studios for sessions due to start at about 10 P.M. and the boys wouldn't arrive until maybe two or three in the morning, pretty much incapable of doing anything."

In September 1967 Oldham got tired of listening to the band playing "deliberately sloppy 12-bar blues," walked out of Olympic, and never came back. It was clear to everyone that the game was over. On September 14 the band told Klein that they'd split with Andrew. The band's new publicist, Les Perrin, released an anodyne statement to the effect that the Stones had parted company with their "recording manager" since they were now capable of producing their own records.

Jagger released his own press statement: "I felt we were doing practically everything ourselves anyway. And we just didn't think along the same lines. Allen Klein is just a financial scene. We'll really be managing ourselves."

This can be read in various ways. Bill Wyman writes, "more accurate would have been an admission by Mick that we were about to be virtually managed by *him*." Now effectively in charge of the day-to-day running of the band, Jagger may also have contemplated taking on the role of producer, but instead he started courting the young American from the Traffic sessions at Olympic, Jimmy Miller. "He asked me to come by that night, to his house on Chester Square in Chelsea," Miller remembers. "Sure enough, he asked me if I'd produce their next album."

The year 1967 ended with the release of *Their Satanic Majesties Request,* an album that gets a lot of favorable mentions these days but sounded confused and out of time on its release. By the spring of 1968 it looked to some people as though the Stones might be washed up. It had been a long while, too, since they had issued an obvious hit single.

The band went back into the studio with their new producer, working on a new album and a single: *Beggars Banquet* and "Jumpin' Jack

Flash." By midsummer 1968 the Stones were back on the English and American singles chart at number 1, and the new album was released late in the year to unanimous critical approval. The Stones entered 1969 right back at the peak of their form.

The improvements in sound and arrangement that Miller brought seem only too obvious when compared today with Oldham's productions. Oldham had never really served in the studio anyway—his forte was publicity—and he'd done such a fine job on the Stones that he'd made himself redundant.

Business Reorgani-zation

And so it was as the new decade began that the Stones, makers of countless hit singles and best-selling albums, indisputably one of the top two rock acts in the world, discovered they were virtually bankrupt. Bill Wyman, the most conservative, practical—and along with Charlie Watts the lowest-earning—member of the band, discovered in 1970 that he owed nearly £120,000 in back taxes.

The coffers did not contain enough to settle the band's total tax bill, and with income tax at 83 percent on the pound on earned income and 98 percent on unearned income, any attempt to generate the money by touring and selling new records would simply create a larger tax bill. Catch-22. After years of runaway success, the Stones were broke.

How did one of the most famous bands in the world ever reach a state where, after eight years of hit records, they were virtually bankrupt? It's a complicated story—or perhaps it's actually a very simple story, deliberately obfuscated by those whose interests are best served by a mass of complications. Like many music-biz stories of the period, it involves Allen Klein. A little bit of flim-flam goes a long way.

Here's the authorized version, as told in 1972 by Mick Jagger to Roy Carr of *New Musical Express,* shortly before the release of *Exile on Main St.:*

> Most bands have this happy-go-lucky attitude about money, which I had for eight years. I just don't worry about it. And no manager I ever had worried about taxes. . . . So after working for eight years I discovered at the end that nobody had ever paid my taxes and I owed a fortune. So then you have to leave the country. So I said fuck it, and left the country.

You'll notice that Jagger speaks as though he's still just a passive observer; one of the boys. In 1972 the majority rock audience didn't want its artists being businessmen. The John Lennon economic model—faceless gray men in gray suits rip off the artist—was by far the most popular view (regardless of the fact that by 1972, even in the more naturally conservative American music-biz, the smarter part of the business spoke, drank, snorted, smoked, and dressed much like the artists they represented).

What you see above is a classic example of Jagger presenting the suitable face for the occasion. He's just the plain old lead singer with the Stones. A lesser individual might have felt tempted to boast about the (considerable) part he'd played in turning things around, but not Jagger. Relatively few readers of *New Musical Express* would have been interested in company restructuring, and plenty would have been ready to start pointing fingers at the Capitalist Pig, but Jagger's infallible instinct for the appropriate persona never falters.

Piecing together facts and information three decades old, the figures vary wildly, but the problem remains clear. The Stones' Decca recordings had generated anywhere between $10 and $100 million (according to your source), yet the band had only received around $1.25 million from Klein.

The New York company he'd set up in 1965—to handle the advance and subsequent payments from U.S. Decca (and to help circumvent U.K. taxes)—bore a similar name to the Stones' English company, Nanker Phelge Music, Ltd., but had one major difference. The sole controller of New York's Nanker Phelge Music, Inc. was Allen Klein. A gulf had been created between the Stones and their income, with Klein as the only bridge. Now, whenever the Stones wanted some of their own money, they had to apply to Klein.

Klein had quickly gone to work on any existing deals, renegotiating some, ignoring others, bulldozing his way through the numerous sources from which a successful band derives income. He'd tied up every possible source of revenue, from the massive recording and publishing receipts down to the rights to sell the 50 cent official tour programs. The Stones' percentages undoubtedly increased, but the benefit all flowed in one direction.

As Jagger went to work reorganizing the London office, everything returned to the same basic problem. To obtain even small sums of money, it was necessary to apply to Klein's New York office—which in practice meant sending telexes, making phone calls, writing letters, sending more telexes—over and over until some money arrived. The Stones were unable to sign their own checks; things got so bad that their office on Maddox St. was in danger of having the electricity cut off.

With everything routed via New York, Klein could procrastinate indefinitely. In a classic control move, Klein would frequently refuse to disburse funds, choosing instead to "lend" the group money. In *True Adventures of the Rolling Stones,* Stanley Booth quotes a memo from Jo Bergman (who ran the band's London office) listing the most immediate problems—band's personal accounts overdrawn, Rolling Stones number 3 account overdrawn, £7,000 needed to clear most pressing debts, no funds available for running office, and so on.

Relationships within the Stones were always tense—and any statement should be examined in the light of who is making it—but some interesting opinions appear in Bill Wyman's book *Stone Alone.* Wyman suggests that Jagger/Richards had an easier time under the new régime than the rest of the band (of course, as songwriters they would have earned far more money). He also suggests that, once Jagger took the helm, the constant problems obtaining small sums of money was one of the methods used to wear down Brian Jones. He cites several instances where the former bandleader appears to have been deliberately humiliated over sums as small as $300.

At this distance it is impossible to assess such claims. One school of thought holds that Brian was such a pain that anyone would have reacted against him, while another maintains that Brian was systematically ground down until he was no threat to the ruling axis, then still further into regions that bordered on punishing him for ever having been in control. Who can say? All we will ever know with any certainty is that soon after leaving the band Brian drowned, in July 1969.

By 1968 Klein was ideally positioned, holding all the cards, his rivals confounded and at each others' throats. In the English courts, large sums of the band's money were frozen by the official receiver, pending the outcome of Eric Easton's lawsuit against his ex-partner Andrew Oldham for breach of contract, and against Klein for inducing Easton's clients to break the contract. (Easton *had* been ruthlessly dumped.) Meanwhile, in a separate suit, Andrew Oldham (now *himself* having been ditched by the Stones, and therefore acting solely on his own behalf) was suing Klein over his sleight-of-hand move that led to the creation of the two Nanker Phelge companies. With dozens more unconnected cases going through the American courts, Klein's moves were cloaked by an impenetrable smoke-screen—perfect operating conditions for a man busy working on as many fronts as Allen Klein.

Band members had different methods of dealing with the Klein cash-flow problem. When Keith Richards needed £20,000 to close the purchase of a house on Cheyne Walk, he simply put the Stones' minder and chauffeur Tom Keylock on a plane to New York, with orders not to return until he had the money. Keylock marched straight into Klein's inner office, past protesting secretaries, and sat himself down facing Klein. He announced the sum of money needed and its purpose. While Klein blustered, Keylock announced his intention to remain in the seat until the money was forthcoming. After about an hour Klein folded and paid up. Keith got his house.

——

Jagger had always mingled with the Chelsea crowd, that mixture of haute bohemia and fashionable society. At one or other of the many parties he'd been introduced to a gentleman merchant banker and *mittel*-European aristocrat, Prince Rupert zu Loewenstein. A wit and an accomplished mimic in at least four languages, Prince Rupert was managing director of an old established merchant bank, Leopold Joseph. Initially Prince Rupert acted as Jagger's financial adviser, and later agreed to represent the whole band, once Klein was no longer in control.

Prince Rupert's advice to Jagger, as the two men went over the books (such as they were), was stark but simple. He concluded that the only real alternatives to filing for bankruptcy were an immediate break with Klein (essential at almost any cost) and a radical strategy to deal with the problem of taxes.

The Stones' Decca contract was about to expire, and several major labels were interested in signing them. The Stones were lucky that at this crucial moment Klein's attention was elsewhere. The Beatles were squabbling amidst the ruins of Apple, and Klein saw his chance to snatch the main prize. Undistracted, Klein would probably have dragged out negotiations with the Stones for years, but at this moment he was prepared to let them go as long he got the money—*all* the money—and the copyrights to the Stones back catalogue as well.

The amount of money the Stones lost (and continue to lose, as more and more of their 1960s hits appear in television commercials) is incalculable, but the settlement did gain them their freedom from Klein. The details are, of course, far more complex than the brief outline given here—a full account of the suits and countersuits would fill several volumes.

Prince Rupert took over as the band's business manager, and Jagger, confident that he had at last found competent advice, began to see the formation of Rolling Stones Records as a real possibility. The appointment of Prince Rupert marks the definitive moment in the evolution of the modern Rolling Stones. With their finances in safe hands, Jagger could take full control of the commercial direction of the band. The success of the arrangement is demonstrated by the band's ever-increasing wealth. Prince Rupert is still the Stones' business manager and—with the Stones as current clients—is naturally unable to discuss any details of their affairs.

On July 30, 1970, a press release announced that Klein would no longer act on behalf of the Stones. The following day the Stones' contract with Decca Records (London Records in the United States) expired. Among the many freedoms gained, Mick Taylor now ceased to be an employee and was awarded his commission as a full Rolling Stone.

Upon the formation of Rolling Stones Records, the Stones had to deliver their old material to Klein. Nina Antonia quotes Jimmy Miller:

> Because of the deal they had with Klein, he owned the rights to all the unused material that they had recorded during their time with him and he'd requested that we make up a reel of all the tracks. Mick said, "I know what he's going to do with it, he's going to put it out. The reason why we didn't finish them was because they weren't good enough. We don't want him releasing them to make every penny he can. Legally we've got to let him hear it, so we want to do session mixes, but it's not meant to sound good." I asked him who was going to engineer it. "You are."

With a gratifyingly low-grade tape run off for Klein, there was still one outstanding task. To complete their contract with Decca, the Stones still had to deliver one last single. Jimmy Miller continues the story. "At the end of the night Mick said, 'I've got this song that would be the pièce de résistance. Can you fix up a mic? I'm going to try an acoustic.' We mic'd him up, and he recorded 'Cocksucker Blues.'"

Known in polite circles as "Schoolboy Blues," the recording is just Jagger and his acoustic guitar—no band, no arrangement, and no production beyond Jimmy Miller riding the reverb control; just a rough, studio demo. Over sparse minor chords, Jagger moans and whines in his most slovenly voice about the trials of a "lonesome schoolboy," new to London and trying to find gainful employment as a rent-boy.

Picture the weekly meeting in the listening room at Decca, with all the heads of departments present around the table, auditioning the week's new single releases, deciding which ones will be plugged and which ones buried. The tape (or acetate) of the new Stones single is lined up, and the executives sit back, waiting to hear a new "Jumpin' Jack Flash" or "Honky Tonk Women."

Instead, the sound that greets them is Jagger's unaccompanied voice, leering at them in an insinuatingly intimate manner, "Well I'm a lone-e-e-e-e-e-e-e-some schoolboy." This does not sound quite right. Is it the correct track? Is it the B side? No? Oh, well, perhaps it picks up in a minute. And it does. Reaching his strongest voice for the chorus, Jagger bellows, "Where can I get my ass fucked? Where can I get my cock sucked?" It's a riot. Jagger plays it dead straight, only once—almost—cracking up, on the words "way too tight" at the end of the third verse.

Sir Edward Lewis's response has not been preserved for posterity, but legally the Stones were free. A final single had been delivered and the contract fulfilled to the letter of the law. Decca's term had expired.

Prince Rupert's second recommendation—a strategy to deal with the years of unpaid taxes—was that the band should go into tax exile. They should absent themselves from England not later than the start of the new tax year, on April 5, 1971.

This took some digesting. England was their home. Most of the band had decent-sized houses in the English countryside, and some had young families. America was always fun, whether on tour or just visiting, but they were always pleased to get back to England. It was the alien quality, the very strangeness of America that made visiting such fun. Living there was another matter.

Loewenstein recommended France. To Jagger, who was conducting an affair with the Paris-based Bianca, this sounded like an attractive option.

France was close to England, and an established colony of English tax exiles already existed there, most of them domiciled on the Riviera.

The stretch of coast that runs from St. Tropez through Cannes, Antibes, Nice, and up to Villefranche was seriously *smart*. The tone had been set by Russian archdukes—the oil magnates of their day—who started wintering at Nice in the 1890s. By 1920 a sizeable number of the American and European rich traveled there for the season. A particular form of smart English life centered on Cap-Ferrat, where the author Somerset "Willie" Maugham had set up home in 1926, partly to avoid tax, partly to escape England for more personal reasons. Close to the casinos of Monte Carlo, the whole Riviera was within easy reach of the cultural treasure of Italy and the medical and financial centers of Switzerland, and it offered a wonderful Mediterranean climate.

Band reactions varied. Some were dubious, others stunned. Some had to consider the serious implications of maintaining large drug habits with supply lines dangerously stretched over 600 miles and an international border. Charlie and his wife Shirley were the most reluctant to abjure the Realm. Keith and Anita were the slowest to actually get there, although inevitably once they did arrive, their house quickly became the center of activity.

The move also spelled the end of a particular form of Chelsea life. Up and down the King's Road, a whole subcommunity of haberdashers, shoemakers, hangers-on, and dope-dealers whose spiritual life focused on the Stones, suddenly found themselves adrift. When I moved into that area in 1975, fading traces of that scene were still discernible—attractive girls in mansion flats whose curtains remained drawn all year round snorted heroin and spoke wistfully of former glories. Boutique owners, dodgy car mechanics, heavies, and men who could Get Things Done, people who'd subsisted around the Stones, either overdosed or ended up going to work for Led Zeppelin. The Stones had been gone four years, but there was still a dying glimmer of a once glamorous scene.

Goodbye Britain

Before the Stones left for France, they had business to conduct. On March 4, 1971 their office announced they were leaving England. On the same day, they began a short farewell tour of England at Newcastle City Hall. Between March 4 and March 14 they played Manchester, Coventry, Glas-

gow, Bristol, Brighton, Liverpool, and Leeds, finishing up in London at the Roundhouse, a famous converted railway shed.

This was a very different band from the crew who stumbled through the shambles at Hyde Park in July 1969. The core five-piece lineup of Jagger, Richards, Watts, Wyman, and Taylor was unchanged, but they'd tightened themselves up beyond measure. Two horns—Jim Price (trumpet and trombone) and Bobby Keys (saxes)—had become regular members of the touring band in late 1970, and they were joined on this tour by Nicky Hopkins, who alternated at the piano with Ian Stewart. This was not a standard issue two-guitar-bass-and-drums beat group with a couple of extra pieces tacked on, but a full-throated, eight-piece rock 'n' roll combo.

Simply adding horns and keyboard doesn't make a combo, it just makes eight people jamming. The key lies in good arrangements—and some of the songs had very good arrangements indeed. What the Stones were approaching at this point was something new, an approach to hard rock that was entirely modern yet rooted in 1950s rock 'n' roll and 1930s–1940s swing.

Charlie Watts is very clearly a big-band swing drummer at heart. His innate understanding of the way that the various sections of a combo inter-act and the role of the drummer in conducting them was plain. Crisp, pow-erful, and understated, he drove the band or sat out with equal poise.

Back in 1972, Keith remembered one show in particular from this 1971 tour. "Bristol was a gas," he told *Melody Maker.* This I must admit is gratifying, since I was there—and it was a gas. It has always remained in mind as the best Stones show I ever saw. However, we are all lucky that the Leeds University show, four days later, was recorded for broadcast by BBC radio, and good quality stereo tapes have been in circulation for years.

Keith and Anita may have been a pain to organize, missing trains and delaying schedules as reported in *Rolling Stone,* but onstage Keith was hav-ing fun. Just as Dylan deliberately rearranged some of his most familiar material on his 1966 tour, so the Stones played around with the familiar. The game was seeing how long it took you to nail the tune. One of their biggest hits of the 1960s started out with just a drum beat, very like Roy Orbison's "Oh, Pretty Woman." In came a guitar playing a spare, funky rhythm part built around 7th chords. Jagger entered, repeating, "Um yeah—thass awrite." The whole thing was reminiscent of one of those holding patterns the Otis Redding Band used to vamp on when the boss was getting ready to testify. At about the 45-second mark, Jagger began singing "Satisfaction." Listening to the tapes today, it's fairly obvious—the element of surprise is lost forever—but at the time it was edge-of-the-seat stuff. It gripped you. Just like a young band should.

Mick Taylor was no longer the shy figure of Hyde Park. He had found his place and was at his graceful, fluent best, alert to everything that was happening onstage, and playing at the top of his form. I'm not sure I've ever seen him play better. There were none of the rambling, overextended solos that mark his later days in concert with the band. Whether using fin-gers, or playing bottleneck on the same regular-tuned guitar, his solos are never extraneous or overblown. He'd settled into the band and none of his later discontentment was evident. I think that, musically at least, these were probably his happiest times: certainly the later period, as things fell to bits around the *Goat's Head Soup* era, can't have been much fun to be around.

Keith by now had perfected his 5-string, open-G style—there were none of the tuning problems and frantic movement of capos up and down the neck that characterized his open-tuned Gibson Flying V at the Hyde Park concert—and was directing the band better than ever from his rhythm-guitar position, stage left of Charlie's drum riser. Setting the tempos and conducting the arrangements, the sound of the open-tuned rhythm guitar (rare in rock music, and almost unheard of then) imparted that inimitable Stones sound to the songs.

Charlie was locked in tight to Keith's guitar, Bill Wyman was slap on the beat of Charlie's bass drum, and Jagger was magnificent. In these days he was still singing rather than devoting the greater part of his energies to calisthenics, like the leader of an aerobics class. As he's aged, he seems to have felt compelled to demonstrate his undiminished fitness—commendable in an athlete, but an exercise that leaves him short of breath. If you listen to a progression of live shows through the 1970s, you can hear the point at which he begins gabbling, hustling through the lyric, foreshortening lines, and sacrificing both phrasing and melody, purely in the interest of running about. Stand still that man.

His time with the Living Theatre had been well spent too. Today the belt-whipping stage routine of Midnight Rambler has become as familiar as old boots, but the first time it was unexpected and highly effective. Truman Capote suggested that, rather than being a highly charged piece of sexual theatre, Jagger was actually whipping a mental image of Prince Rupert in order to encourage him to count the gate receipts—but that may have been wishful thinking on Capote's part. Capote also described the 1972 model Jagger as being "about as sexy as a pissing toad," so perhaps his point of view was not entirely neutral.

By spring 1971 the expanded band was firing on all cylinders, and that energy carried over into the summer when work began on the new album. The band that went into the studio was a tight, road-tested outfit, familiar with each other's playing in a way that no amount of preproduction or rehearsal-studio work can ever produce.

I think many of the clues to *Exile*'s greatness were visible in those shows. The set was well selected, beautifully paced, and nicely sequenced.

Here was an experienced band at the very peak of its power, swinging, and obviously having a lot of fun. Like anything, bands have their seasons, and 1971 was high summer for the Rolling Stones. Within the month they were off to France, where they'd record an album provisionally titled *Tropical Disease.*

That album became *Exile on Main St.*

INTERLUDE

A Conversation with Anita Pallenberg

In the spring of 1971 Anita, Keith, and the rest of the Stones had to leave England, once the *Goodbye Britain* tour was completed. Preparations to get the band out of England before the start of the new tax year on April 5 were in hand. Office supremo Jo Bergman already had houses rented in the south of France, and truckloads of personal possessions in transit.

Several members of the Stones were reluctant to abandon their settled English lifestyles, but none had as much to fear as Keith and Anita. For them, the major problem in moving to a new country—one, moreover, in which they had no connections—was getting off smack. Neither had left England for any length of time since developing serious habits, and both were reluctant to leave their comfortable, cocooned nest in Cheyne Walk.

There was no getting around the move to France, however. As the critical date grew nearer, the couple carried on as normal, ignoring the deadline, though even Keith's legendary stubbornness and intractability weren't going to be of much assistance in this crisis. Both partners were addicted beyond the point where a move to France and five or six days sweating it out would answer. With an eighteen-month-old child to look after (Marlon), it made sense to undergo treatment one at a time.

Keith went first. On March 15, the day after the Stones' final show at the Roundhouse, he retreated to his country house, Redlands, under the care of "Smitty," a tough old girl who had been nurse and assistant to the noted Dr. Dent, advocate of the Apomorphine cure. Keith's choice of

31

cure is telling—the outlaw rocker instinctively turned to the celebrated literary outlaw Lonesome Cowboy Bill, Mr. William Burroughs.

Burroughs's combination of intelligence, dry avuncular wit, and long practical experience granted him legendary status at the literary end of the junk world, or more precisely at the junkie end of the literary world. His best-known work, *The Naked Lunch* (required reading in respectable underground circles), contains an appendix reprinted from *The British Journal of Addiction,* volume 53, number 2, entitled "Letter from a Master Addict to Dangerous Drugs," in which Burroughs contrasts the various worthless cures he'd undergone with the efficacy of Dent's method.

Dr. John Yerbury Dent had built up an impressive practice since the 1940s, discreetly curing the upper classes and well-to-do bohemians of a variety of drink and drug problems—but unfortunately for Keith, Dent was no longer alive. Luckily, after his death, Smitty—who was married to a South-London police sergeant—carried on the work, regardless of her legal status, as a nurse.

Keith's all-purpose assistant, Spanish Tony, drove him to Redlands and collected him again, ten days later. In his book *Ups and Downs with the Rolling Stones,* Tony Sanchez describes the newly cleaned-up Keith as "battered and pale" but possessing all the "exuberance of a man who has just been freed from jail." After some stock passages about withdrawals, designed to make the reader's flesh crawl, he describes Smitty administering Keith a "morphine substitute"—in fact, it would have been Apomorphine, Dr. Dent's sovereign remedy, a substance that has no opiate effect whatever.

Opinions differ about the efficacy of Apomorphine. Keith called the cure "pretty medieval," while a gentleman of my acquaintance who was twice treated by Dent for alcoholism described his method as "straightforward aversion therapy." By contrast, William Burroughs considered it a panacea so effective that it was deliberately sidelined by a powerful cabal of vested interests.

A lot of rot is talked about the scale of Keith's habit around the time of *Exile* and the subsequent summer 1972 U.S. promotional tour. Stanley Booth, who was with Keith at many of the key moments—and a man who knows his way around a pharmacy—insists that in 1972 Keith was mostly snorting the drug, "though the toots were of a size to sedate a Kentucky Derby winner, but it wasn't as bad as it was gonna get."

Keith with Telecaster, 1972. The defining image of 1970s rock. (PHOTO: LAURENS VAN HOUTEN, STAR FILE)

It's plain that a constitution as strong as that of the 29-year-old Richards would, under any régime, have sailed through the worst of the withdrawals in ten days. Had he chosen to he could have turned his back on the drug there and then (changing the whole iconography of rock!), but of course that's not the way it went. Back in London, Keith set about consuming speedballs (a heroin and cocaine mixture) with all the added pleasure that follows a period of abstinence.

When he did take to the needle full time, Keith injected his heroin intramuscularly (skin-popping)—which accounts for the interesting pattern of ridges and valleys still visible on his upper arms—rather than going for intravenous hits (mainlining). And, highly unusual among needle users, he usually snorted his coke, reckoning that this was the safest and healthiest combination. Stanley Booth's statement, that Keith was still a long way from the real depths, is supported by the mainlining scene and the subsequent nod shown in Robert Frank's film *Cocksucker Blues*—few regular mainline shooters would have passed out in quite that fashion.

On his second day back in London, while Anita began her detox at Bowden House (a well-known clinic at Harrow-on-the-Hill) and the Stones were filming television footage at the Marquee, the newly energized Keith Richards used his Gibson to take a swing at the head of club owner Harold Pendleton, whose insistence on prominently displaying a large sign reading "The Marquee" was interfering with the filming. Keith missed his target and a possible charge of grievous bodily harm.

At Bowden House, Anita's treatment wasn't going so well. Since the making of *Performance* in autumn 1968, she'd gradually become more addicted than Keith, filling the time while the band was away on the road, hanging out with Marianne Faithfull, reading Robert Graves's *The White Goddess,* and skin-popping speedballs three or four times a day.

Eventually the couple moved to France, where they took up residence in a large house named Villa Nellcôte, standing on a hill above the fishing village of Villefranche-sur-Mer.

Anita Pallenberg: I was clean when I first arrived at Nellcôte.

John Perry: But feeling pretty fragile . . .

AP: Oh yeah! Well I'd done that thing, which in those days they called a "Sleeping Cure." Out of all the cures I'd tried, that was the one I did at the time. Which was where they put you to sleep for seven days, and you go through withdrawals sleeping—or you're *supposed* to, at least.

JP: Any good?

AP: Well in my case . . . first, I had Spanish Tony always coming with a gram of coke, and then it just didn't work. I was just bashing my head. And there were all these really sharp corners by the bed, so I was bruising myself all over, and eventually—you know—I just took off.

And then, I think they gave me Heminevrin,* in those days that was very big as well, and I just gave up and thought "I'll detox privately." I tried doing it with coke—which was THE WORST thing I've ever done in my life!

JP: I see the logic, but in practice it'd only intensify the symptoms.

AP: Oh yeah, yeah, exactly. The logic was that it would numb you, right?

JP: The *logic*'s fine . . .

AP: It's amazing the way your brain starts to think, you know? [laughter]

JP: So you arrived in France, what, in late April?

AP: I'd just come out from Bowden House and the first days when we got out there, with the Mistral, that hot wind, *howling* through the chimneys, and there's just me and Keith set up camp there . . . I felt spooked out. I was very, very spooked out. Like a premonition of what was to come, a feeling, a foretaste of coming disaster. [laughter] But then the album, as you see, turned out the best.

Villa Nellcôte was built for a retired English Admiral with a taste for horticulture, and the gardens and terraces were full of trees, plants, and bushes brought back by nautical friends from all corners of the globe.

AP: Villefranche was this great deep-water harbor. The U.S. Sixth Fleet used to put in there. And when the fleet came in the whole village opened up. The sailors immediately took tons of acid and would then just *rage* through the town; I think one day there was even some shooting. Wild days. I mean these guys, after they stopped at Villefranche, would go down to Istanbul and that's where they got all the hash and things—they were always loaded.

In the early days, before anything was properly arranged, you know, me and Bobby Keys built a raft. I remember one night rowing out and trying to see what

---

* Heminevrin is the trade name of the hypnotic drug Chlormethiazole. It is more usually associated with recovering alcoholics, though in the early 1970s medical fashions may have been different. It was an overdose of this drug that killed Keith Moon in 1978. The drug remains in the British National Formulary.

was goin' on. We used to do that lots, rowing out in the night . . . check the Americans out, shoutin' up to the sailors, see what they had.

And then the Germans, I remember the German U-boats would come up on the surface, and you'd hear—see, nobody was allowed onshore but the Americans, they were the only ones to be given shore leave, and the Germans had to stay on their boats out in the bay—so in the middle of the night you'd hear somebody playing flute across the water. It was haunting . . . and kinda romantic too. But I always liked sailors anyway, so there you go!

Then Keith got this boat, a Riva. He'd drive the boat like a car. The most harrowing thing of all was Keith driving the boat. Outings on the boat. Everybody was terrified he was gonna blow himself up. I just put my hands over my ears . . .

Noted on several continents for his unorthodox motoring style, Keith evidently felt equally unconstricted by conventional nautical precepts. The risk of death or injury does not appear to have affected his notions of seafaring. Several of the kids in the party liked to ride in the boat, and after sighting a couple of Keith's early voyages, Ian Stewart took aside Carol Price (wife of trumpeter Jim Price) and told her in his usual blunt terms that it would be wiser in future to keep her 5-year-old son Mark well away from any boat with Keith at the helm.

AP: It was the way he'd drive over the rocks—he thought he was on a highway. It was so scary the way he took off, with all these rocks *just* protruding a little bit above the sea. He used to just skip' em by the inch—sometimes, I don't know, he flew over them or, I dunno, it was kinda almost like magic. A magic carpet, flying over the sea. And the waves, he didn't know how to ride the waves—he didn't know *anything*, he'd just drive it like a car.

JP: I imagine the house was huge . . . great high ceilings.

AP: Nellcôte had been, in the war you know, a big Nazi headquarters. There were still swastikas on the old heating system, and in every door there were mirrors—I don't know if you've seen the pictures? All the doors had mirrored panels, and you could set the doors in a certain way so you could look around corners. I remember you could sit in the living room and look into the kitchen, all through the hall, to the entrance. Mirror games—like *Performance* again, you know? It was kind of playing with reflections a lot. Otherwise, upstairs it was long corridors and a flight of rooms, all chintzy kind of stuff.

Firstly I reopened the kitchen that had been closed for a hundred years, decorated it, got the Aga going again, and I remember Marshall Chess [head of Rolling Stone Records at the time] saying, "If you pull through, when you've finished all this, I'll give you a Ferrari." Just to thank me for all the trouble I was putting myself through, 'cause I mean, the food was actually the major problem. You couldn't always just run into town and buy food for all these people, you know, everybody would be hungry at different times. Sometimes there'd be twenty people sitting down. . . . I think we had one big meal at lunch, like two, three o'clock in the afternoon, then everybody was on their own really. I never saw the Ferrari!

We had one of those big open gangster cars, a Citroën. That was our attempt to kind of fit in with the locals. We went up in the hills once and lost a wheel, almost killed ourselves. That was really scary. And Keith had his Jag . . . there was that trouble down at the harbor but I wasn't there when that happened.

On May 26, Keith got into a scuffle with an Italian motorist and the Beaulieu harbormaster. It threatened to escalate into something more serious when Keith helped matters along by producing one of Marlon's toy guns. Spanish Tony appears to have saved the immediate situation (see *Ups and Downs with the Rolling Stones,* pp. 238–239), though legal matters rumbled on until December, when the French magistrate dismissed the charges.

On June 3, even the Watts family managed to fall foul of traditional Anglo-French relations. Charlie's wife, Shirley—probably tired and overemotional from the flight—got into a shouting match with French customs at Nice Airport. In due course (and in absentia), a short prison sentence was handed down and later suspended.

AP: Soon after we arrived, we had this hassle with the local hoods trying to threaten us—I was the only French speaker, remember—so we thought, rather than fight them, employ them. Big mistake, obviously. We put a couple of them to live in the gatehouse, they were supposed to be security, and took on this guy Jacques as the cook—the scene that escalated into all the trouble at the end. It never really occurred to me that we were so disliked—it's bizarre, isn't it? I mean there was almost more of us than there was of them!

JP: Anita, the old story about the power for the recording truck being nicked from the electric railway lines—true?

AP: Yup.

Anita clearly wasn't going to enlarge on this, though obviously it would have been no more her domain than lining up the heads on the recording console. However, the image of Anita and Bobby Keys in camouflage suits—faces daubed with Revlon Night-Fighter makeup, midnight creeping through the maquis with rolls of high-power cable over their shoulders and crocodile clips clenched in their teeth—is nearly as irresistible as the thought of a modern French Rolling Stones tour sponsored by the S.N.C.F. (Société Nationale des Chemins de Fer, the French national railroad company).

After years of working on booked time at commercial studios, Keith now had the working songwriter's dream setup, a professional-quality recording studio under the eaves of his own house. If he woke up at four in the afternoon with a riff going around in his head, he only had to wander down to his basement to put the idea straight onto master tape. A casual glance at the credits on the *Exile* sleeve can be misleading. The natural assumption is to picture the full band all playing together in the basement. Not so. Only eight of the eighteen tracks feature the five Stones playing their own instruments. The rest consist of Keith plus whoever happened to be around the house at the time: Keith's songs, Keith's house, Keith's album. It's no coincidence that the Nellcôte regulars— Keith, Jimmy Miller, Mick Taylor, and Bobby Keys—are the ones who feature most prominently.

AP: Days when they were *all* together down in the basement were actually not that often, you know. Musicwise it'd be just going on and on. Sometimes there'd be just Mick there, and sometimes there'd be just Keith. Other times the band, it was almost nonstop. When the whole band was playing it was pretty loud—you could hear it clearly in the Square at Villefranche. Andy Johns would be sitting out there in the truck for hours and hours—at any time, day or night. Where did he stay? Did he stay at our house?

JP: Probably slept in the truck. Sounds like he was on 24-hour call.

AP: Yeah, yeah it was 24-hour call. I spent time in the truck and in the basement, but the tracks that I remember . . . that kinda Samba feel I liked in those days—

JP: "Sweet Black Angel"?

AP: Yeah, that's the one. I always used to go down there and dance. Dedicated to Angela Davis. We were all into that stuff, into the Chicago Eight and all that shit, it was the big thing at the time. Pretty interesting period.

Anita points to a photo on the wall of her Chelsea flat: Allen Ginsberg, Tom Hayden, and other figures of the day, marching in support of the Chicago Eight.

Mick Jagger and Keith Richards backstage at Madison Square Garden, 1972 US tour. (PHOTO: JOE SIA, STAR FILE)

AP: But otherwise I was too busy trying to keep the whole place together.

JP: There are some great pictures of Gram Parsons and Keith playing in the upstairs rooms.

AP: There was always jamming going on, you know . . . upstairs, downstairs. Mick sometimes was on his own, and Keith refused to go down. It was always like [growly voice] "I'm not gonna go down there." Keith always likes to give Mick a hard time, you know.

Even when we were in Switzerland . . . Mick had come to Switzerland with like, PEN and PAPER, to WRITE some SONGS, you know? So then, he'd come to the house and he'd sit there. We'd be knocked out, and Keith would wake up at like five in the afternoon, and Mick had been there since eleven o'clock, you know, twiddling his thumbs. When Keith eventually got up at five and then he'd get in the bath for another couple of hours . . . Mick was really slagging him off. And it's just because they've got two ways of working. Mick likes to write black and white, ABC; with Keith it's just getting a feeling. Mick likes to write "brrrrrrrm" [imitates typewriter] and Keith is just like, all about *sound.* He plays what he hears and knocks up a song when it comes. So, a lot of that was going on and Gram was always a bit like pig in the middle.

Gram had been around since the English tour in March. As Keith told the *New York Rocker:*

> There's not a lot of guys you don't mind waking up and they're there—for weeks—and it's a pleasure to have them around. For me, Gram was a way of getting a bit outside of the Stones, which was getting very claustrophobic in those years. It was very nice to have another musician, a writer, just to bounce ideas over, without any sense of intrusion.

Andy Johns told the same paper that Gram

> was there nearly all the time. He was a very nice, pleasant, true fellow. Very out of it though. I remember one time [him] sitting on a Vox amplifier with a foot pedal up to his ear thinking it was a pair of earphones going, "Yeahhh, Tuuuuuuuuuuuuuuuuumbl-ing De-ice." It was really terrible, man. Poor fellow. In the kitchen that was, too. We did quite a bit of recording in the kitchen.

JP: Gram doesn't seem to be on the record.

AP: I don't think Gram even went down there.

JP: The impression is that Jagger resented Gram getting too friendly with Keith.

AP: He was the other side of the coin, you know? There's always that other stuff goin' on—whoever's the one that they're all always going on about. Boys will be boys, I guess. So Gram was on that end of it, you know, and Taylor on the other end of it . . . poor Mick. He was very, uuhhhh, very *torn,* you know? The whole thing was a nightmare. Aggression. Sexual aggression. It was like aggression on every bloody level. Taylor was constantly harassed by Jagger, in every way. I remember seeing him in tears.

JP: Yeah, I heard stuff along those lines . . . Jagger comin' on to Rose—

AP: Coming on to *Taylor*—you know, Jagger's bisexual—just giving him a hard time any possible way he could. It certainly wasn't easy for poor Mick [Taylor]. Some days he was too scared to go down to the basement . . . he'd lie in bed and chill out—hide under the pillows!

But then I thought that, out of all of them, Mick Taylor was like the most open-minded one, you know? I remember one morning going into his room and he was lying there in bed with Rosie and he said, "Oh, Anita, why don't you jump into bed with us?" Which was something that none of the others would have *ever . . .* [laughter] I mean, nothing happened, but . . . it kind of impressed me at the time!

JP: During that time you were in France, Keith started to come to the fore. In the beginning, the bandleader was Brian. Mick was the one out front, but the *focus* was Brian—he seemed years ahead. He dressed better. And those sly little smiles at the camera . . .

AP: Yep.

JP: Then the focus shifted to Mick. His confidence grew, and one just accepted it as Mick's band. But around the time of that long Greenfield interview with Keith in *Rolling Stone,* it seemed—

AP: Keith.

JP: Yeah, was when Keith came through . . .

AP: Yep, yep.

JP: . . .as the heart of the band.

AP: Well, to actually do something like that, to have the recording in his own house, it's quite an extraordinary thing—and a generous commitment too. I'm sure nobody else could have put up with anything like it, on that scale. [laughter] I mean, I know now that other bands, since . . .

Marshall Chess was there as well, he was a . . . house plant. I mean there was some people that just didn't budge! Nicky Hopkins as well, he was there in the house . . . huh huh! . . . Michael Cooper came down. This troupe of musicians arrived at one point, the Bauls of Bengal, all wearing orange robes and their hair done up on top. Took them about a minute to empty the table. Aahhhh, it's all just such vague kind of memories, but you know I never really look at those things too closely 'cause . . . I don't want to, really.

JP: Tracks like "Happy" are just Keith, Jimmy Miller, and Bobby Keys.

AP: Yeah.

JP: There's a guy named Bill Plummer, played upright bass on several tracks.

AP: I can't remember him. Mind you, I can hardly remember seeing Bill Wyman.

JP: Probably one of the players overdubbed in L.A., then.

AP: Mmmm. And then Bianca came a few times as well. She'd arrive, and then she'd disappear for four hours in the bathroom—you know, and we're all kind of wondering. She'd go in with this huge, *massive* makeup bag, and she came out and she looked *totally* the same! She always used the makeup to perfection, but you don't see that it's makeup. It looks completely natural, that fantastically careful makeup that looks like no makeup at all.

Then there was Rosie Taylor . . . that whole thing was another nightmare as well . . . like a sex story going on.

JP: Those were busy days . . . everywhere. [laughter]

AP: I mean Bobby [Keys] was the one most on the prowl, actually—though his wife, Judy, she came down as well at certain points, I remember that.

JP: Bobby Keys was supposed to be sharing a house with Jim and Carol Price, though he seems to have been at your place most of the time. Carol said, "Mick always wanted to go out and be seen. With the right people. Not that Keith didn't like to party . . . but he preferred to do it at home. Keith liked having the wife and kids around. One night Bobby Keys phoned up, said he was going out, wanted me and Jim to come along. It was like a double date—Mick and Bianca, Bobby and Catherine Deneuve. In his best Lubbock, Texas accent Bobby yells, "Ah got me a day-ate with a rill-laahve movie stahhh!"

AP: All that . . . Alain Delon, Nathalie Delon, all those guys were around too. Bobby used to call me "Sweet Magnolia." It was really nice. Sweet Magnolia!

The live album *No Security* is playing on Anita's new stereo.

AP: This is the version of "Sister Morphine," but I don't like it. I don't think he [Jagger] gives the song the right . . . Mick has no empathy for the song. But Marianne [Faithfull] was finally given credit. But then, apparently, 'cause Marianne's been doing this video about her life, and she wanted Mick and Keith on it as well, so she got Mick, and Mick now says that Marianne *didn't* write this song, she just added a few words. So I don't know whether they'll cut that out, or what happened, but that's the grapevine.

JP: OK. I remember a scene in the mid-eighties, at Right Track studio, Marianne was using, I dunno, I think it was some Stones downtime, early November '85. Mike Thorne producing. As I understood it, nobody was sure when the Stones were going to show up . . . and she always left the studio early, 'cause she didn't wanna

risk bumping into him, even in the elevator. So Marianne will speak to Mick now, will she?

AP: Yeah, she does . . . but he doesn't particularly wanna speak to her.

JP: The band sounds *good* on this.

AP: That's what Keith does, you know, he keeps Mick going by getting really good musicians. Otherwise, if it was left to him, Mick would trash it. That's Mick's personality, he likes to say, "Oh yeah, Keith, he's my guitar player."

The album plays on, and Anita pulls out odds and ends, pictures, mementos.

AP: Pity that I don't have more photographs, material, but you know how it is. I'm sure there's someone sitting somewhere with a *load* of that stuff . . . you know, the Cecil Beaton pictures are all gone [Tangier, 1967], so much *stuff* . . . gone.

Côte d' Azur, May 1971. Left to Right: Marlon Richards, Anita Pallenberg, Spanish Tony, Keith Richards, Jake Webber.
(Photo: Corbis/Bettmann)

Still, some people are putting together a good quality book about *Performance,* you know, good pictures, properly produced.

One wall of Anita's flat contains two pictures from this project, huge blowups of contact sheets. The opposite wall has windows overlooking the Thames, and I wander over to the window, watching the barges on the gray water.

AP: I got very into what was going on in the bay. We had these huge binoculars out on the terrace and we were watching nonstop, 'cause almost every day a new boat would come in—the *Christina,* the *Creole* that belonged to the Onassis brothers.

I got really into boats, we'd go the marina all the time, check out the boats. And then there was the *Zaca,* Errol Flynn's boat, that was moored there, too. We used to go for walks in the afternoons, often end up on the *Zaca,* roam around onboard.

It was a beautiful flat-top three-master—places for parrots—it must've been *incredible* when it was working. The boat was so exotic, all mahogany inside, just beautiful—but with this white washing machine sitting outside on the deck! Keith wanted to buy it, restore it, but nothing came of it.

The schooner belonged to Errol Flynn's son, Sean. Working as photographer in the Vietnam War, he had last been seen riding off toward Cambodia on the back of a motorbike. Keith fancied buying the vessel, but with its owner missing and presumed dead, the mooring fees had mounted up to the point where the whole process would have been a nightmare.

AP: I'm glad nothing came of it; it would've been just one more of those acquisitions, you know?

We got this boat called the *Salamander* which Keith changed to the *Mandrax.** I don't know what happened to the *Mandrax;* I think it eventually ended up in Jamaica . . . I don't think it was seagoing anymore, probably just in storage. Beautiful boat.

We had one rubber dinghy there that was chained to a tree, but the chain got sawn through and it got stolen.

On October 1, while the local "security" men slept in the gatehouse, eleven guitars were stolen from Nellcôte.

---

* Mandrax was the English trade name for Methaqualone, known as Quaalude in the United States. Mandrax was withdrawn from the British National Formulary sometime in the mid-1970s.

AP: Bobby Keys's black sax went as well. Later, I think a few of those pieces turned up in Amsterdam. Somebody had been looking out for them—recovered them—retrieved a few anyway.

JP: Ohhhhh. Losing *one* guitar you care about is bad; all your favorite instruments at one go would be agony.

AP: That was nasty—it was sort of an inside job, you know? Definitely a London job. Tommy Webber—part of that lot. Tommy came down with a whole lot of people; said they'd driven the whole way in Donovan's gypsy caravan [which itself had been stolen, four months earlier, from the 1971 Glastonbury Festival at Pilton, though I don't know whether it was recovered].

JP: Everything came to a halt?

AP: With no guitars I think we did close down for a few days. The wedding [the Jaggers, in May]—we closed down for a few days, and then that incident—we closed down for a bit. And then the whole kinda drama with security, you know . . . blocking the way . . . the massive gates were closed, and big lights shining onto the street. We went to maximum security. Suddenly it became Auschwitz. We were even thinking of putting monkeys in the bread tree to enhance security . . . all sorts of crazy ideas.

But TOO LATE, you know? As usual. Too much trust and faith in everything until you get ripped off. I mean we should've done that before—but that was the time and that was the vibe. We felt like King of the Castle anyway, you know? Nothin' can happen to us. . . .

JP: Spanish Tony mentions the Marseilles guys with the pink smack—

AP: Cotton Candy . . . oh, yeah. Very rare.

JP: Good?

AP: Oh fantastic, yeah. It was totally pure. We had one bag of smack and one bag of cut. Do-it-yourself kind of thing. I mean it was lucky nobody died on the premises really. . . . We were all set to behave, but I remember exactly, they all just came and kept on coming, with masses and masses of stuff. And you can only say "no" so many times.

JP: Well, quite.

Gretchen Parsons told *Rolling Stone* magazine, "The surroundings at Nell-côte were beautiful, but the tension was relentless. You could cut the air with a knife." She probably didn't realize that her figure of speech was about to become literal.

AP: I think just about *everybody* came down to see us, and when they saw that it was like a really loose kind of situation, they just went out to lunch. So what I did, just to scare them, I developed this technique of knife-throwing, you know, just throwing knives at the door from the staircase, to be *threatening.* Somebody would come in, and *pssssssssssswwww!* This knife would go whistling through the hall and stick in the door, just to give 'em a feeling of "Don't fuck with us." But then they still did . . . so there you go.

JP: The Marseilles underworld is a fairly serious proposition.

AP: Yeah, exactly. Thank God these guys went to Marseilles themselves to pick up, it's not like the people from Marseilles came to see us. Like I say, a couple of them came with a half-kilo in the boot [trunk] and we managed to get rid of them . . . but we never went without, it's true.

I remember one day I walked into the living room and there were these two guys sitting there, cowboy hats, cowboy boots—I guess it was the big fashion in those days—and one says, "Oh, we are from Marseilles, we brought you some gifts," and out of the boot came like half a kilo of smack. I said, "No, we don't do that," and kicked them out—it was like . . . there were already massive amounts of stuff floating around.

And among other things I tried again to stop [heroin] with coke. I had this bag, it was at least an ounce of coke, and I thought, if I lock myself in the room, take a lot of coke—you know, it's supposed to numb you—I'm not gonna feel the withdrawals.

JP: Hmmm . . .

AP: I climbed the walls.

JP: Who wouldn't? Once paranoia sets in, you don't know who's trustworthy.

AP: It started to get really scary. By then I started to get *highly* paranoiac, but with paranoia there's always a pinch of reality in there, too. So I remember going around into the garden, 'cause there were all these people who'd, like, invaded the house, and we didn't know who they were. The build-up was nasty. I remember there was a French chick, and there was this handbag. The chick was probably some groupie or something—'cause there was all that shit going on as well—so I looked in the handbag and I saw then that it [contained] a police warrant card.

And then the sneaky way they kind of caught us . . . nobody ever came and raided the place, nobody. Oh, I think once there was a little, a kind of mini-police raid, but there was always something goin' on—so that's why we always had "the drill." Just in case.

Bust drill. From the bedroom, out of the second floor window onto the roof of the recording truck and out into the garden. We had regular rehearsals. 'Cause there was a *vast* amount of drugs there . . . and all these hoods from Marseilles— these guys were dealing from our house, as well, that's what we didn't realize, they were dealing from the premises. That's why we got nailed with all that stuff.

JP: When the situation with the hired locals boiled over?

AP: Within forty-eight hours of firing those guys the trouble started. They went to their mums, their mums made them go to the police and confess and involve everyone in the house. I myself had fourteen years hanging over my head, me and Bobby. I was accused of trafficking. And then all the other people were incriminated as well, but I think me and Bobby Keys, for some reason, were the worst . . . 'cause, I dunno, they probably took a dislike to us. Me, because I fired them, so that was the revenge.

And so we had to just leave, you know, from one day to the other we just had to go. Left the premises. The police, though, never actually came to check . . . they never actually found anything.

And then there were other incriminations, such as, there was this Oliver guy from the Living Theatre, he came down and apparently he slipped some Mandrax to some local youths and tried to rape them . . . so there were all those incriminations of corrupting minors, I mean it was mega-trouble.

And then we just kind of, uhhh . . . ran. We packed our suitcases. We had a dog there called Syph—uh, no, called Okeefenokee the Swamp Dog, a Labrador—and he used to go out on his own walks on the beach, and he got quite popular there. So we thought, well, we might as well leave the dog here. We had a German woman as caretaker and she stayed there, and we paid the rent for the house, £1000 a week, just to keep the dog there.

Retaining an expensive house on French soil was also a smart move as far as the French lawyers were concerned, because it proved intention to return and answer any potential charges arising from the denunciations. While the French police wanted to keep Keith and Anita in the country, their lawyers argued that the extended lease (with an option to buy) was clear proof of the couple's intention to return to France to face any firm charges that may have been drawn up. The argument was accepted, and in November Keith and Anita left the country.

AP: And then eventually the dogs disappeared on the Côte d'Azur, and it all kind of fizzled out. But we actually just had to leave, from one day to the next—it was quite dramatic. We got thrown out to Los Angeles.

JP: How long were you banned from France?

AP: More than five years. The whole thing had to be put to sleep. I think there was one confrontation where me and Keith didn't go, 'cause we were too hot . . . or I didn't go . . . but Mick, and I think maybe Keith, went. Charlie and all the boys went and had to be confronted with Jacques [the cook] and all that lot. And they didn't have the guts to say it face to face. So that was that.

JP: Sounds like a shakedown.

AP: Yeah, yeah, absolutely. I went back there, though now I think it's turned into a kind of parking lot. I haven't been down there lately, but that's what I hear. The whole property was sold and turned into a parking lot. But when I went back, everything was there, there was still the wall, and they had written on it, "Les Rolling Stones Pigs." Like real nasty bloody stuff! [laughter] I thought, "Wow, what a way to be . . . I never really realized that they hated us as much." It was like a weird memory. I'm glad I eventually got out of there.

JP: So the whole French scene started around the time of Mick and Bianca's wedding in May, and turned nasty in less than six months. It could have ended very badly.

AP: Oh yeah. I mean, it didn't help that Bobby Keys was like stirring it up all the time. Going to the casino and picking up people, going to parties and behaving outrageously. I mean, we were like wild people in that house. I mean, even the wedding was like the Wild Bunch. We went to the wedding, and I remember Eric Clapton and his girlfriend came back with us, and they were withdrawing as well, and puking up. It really was, on a daily basis, just a constant drama. Then it always changed as well. People taking advantage of the situation. As I say, this guy raping minors and all that stuff, slipping people pills—things that I didn't even know about were goin' on.

Villefranche to me always had a sort of pirate feel. It was a very romantic kind of place—but ultimately we were unwanted, I guess.

THE SONGS

There are several keys to understanding *Exile on Main St.* Although it's an easy assumption to make when consuming an album, reading the press, and watching video clips, records are not created in a vacuum. The conditions in which the record is made, and the relationships among its makers, tell you a lot about the record itself.

The first key is the growing estrangement between Mick Jagger and Keith Richards; its source, the rift between Bianca Jagger and Anita Pallenberg. When Anita first appeared in Brian Jones's life in 1965, the rest of the band viewed her with considerable suspicion. She was, after all, not only "some foreign bird" but "clever" too—a damning combination. With their straight, 9-to-5 girlfriends, the young Stones may have traveled further than other young men of their own age and background, but they still shared most of their assumptions and prejudices without reservation.

In the course of acting, modeling, and simply hanging out, Anita had seen at least as much of Europe and New York as the Stones and knew a far broader range of society, especially in the worlds of film, fashion, and art. When Jagger attempted to drive her out of the Stones circle, using the type of crude abuse that usually worked with uneducated factory girls and uncertain Pont St. debutantes, he met an altogether less-vulnerable opponent, one with a longer reach (her social connections easily outweighed Jagger's) and a stronger punch (perhaps "squash" is the more appropriate word).

Anita was not about to be put down by some pimply suburban youth. As she says, "Jagger saw me as a threat. But he fell to bits if anyone stood

49

up to him." Keith was still at that stage where he sneered at everything except Chuck Berry and Jimmy Reed, and since it didn't directly affect him, he didn't much care either way.

Spanish Tony's book *Ups and Downs with the Rolling Stones* gives as good an account as any of the high summer of the Jones/Pallenberg Court, where the first alliances were formed between the most fashionable English rock band and the hipper young members of the aristocracy. Each party had something the other wanted. Londoners already acquainted with Anita, people like the antique dealer Christopher Gibbs and gallery owner Robert Fraser, found themselves in the position of power brokers, able to combine business with pleasure while acquiring kudos in the process.

Andrew Oldham disapproved. "I got impatient with all that stuff," he told Philip Norman. "It was like being back at Public School. You had to be in Mick's house or Keith's house or Brian's house. It all started when they got involved with the so-called society people—the Frasers, the Donald Cammells."

Brian and Anita, who were looking more and more like blonde twins, drew an ever-expanding circle into their scene. Gradually Keith started hanging out with them, dropping acid, and mocking the "straight" Mick Jagger (if the word can be applied to someone who was going through another of his camp phases). Soon Keith was living at the flat. For a while the dominant power base was Richards/Jones.

Once Anita left Brian for Keith in mid-1967, and became friends with Jagger's new girlfriend, Marianne Faithfull, the power base shifted for the last time, back to the songwriting team Jagger/Richards, placing Anita right at its center. Mick and Keith plus "the Stones blondes" enjoyed the high ground for the rest of the decade.

Marianne eventually left Jagger—reluctantly, gradually, and after more than one suicide attempt—explaining that his personality was so dominant it left her no room to breathe. She compared the experience to being consumed alive. Sitting on her wall in Soho, smacked into a trance, was positively liberating after what she felt she'd been through in Cheyne Walk.

Not until 1971, when Donald Cammell (writer of the film *Performance*) introduced Jagger to the Nicaraguan-born, Parisian-based socialite, Bianca Pérez Mora Maçias, did the trouble start. Bianca's ruling passion was society, not rock 'n' roll, and Anita thought that Jagger's shared taste for the social ladder was unlikely to help the band rock. Anyway, she hated Bianca.

Claims that she still had her own eye on Jagger can be pretty thoroughly rejected, I think. Anyone who knows Anita's temperament can see how long that relationship would have lasted. She might have been interested in a *contest* with him—by whatever means necessary—but she wouldn't have stood more than a day or two of the social strutting. No, any threat Anita felt was to her position of power as leading lady of the Stones network.

Just as Jagger had resented Anita's entry into the charmed circle, Anita attempted to discourage Bianca. By the time *Exile* was being made, Bianca wouldn't go near Anita—or Villa Nellcôte—so Jagger was reduced to flying back and forth between the studio on the Riviera and Bianca's Parisian circle. As Jagger told *Melody Maker* at the launch, "I was there for a lot of the time in France. I think I was there for at least three of the basic tracks."

The first casualty was the relationship between Mick Jagger and Keith Richards—most crucially, the songwriting relationship—though the results would take another year and another album to show up in the work.

The second point to grasp is the extent to which *Exile* is Keith's album. Instances as pure as this are much rarer in the lives of bands and musicians than one might suppose, and should be treasured when circumstances allow them to occur. The Stones had moved to France, taking separate houses, with the intention of finding a studio somewhere within easy reach of all their homes.

When *Rolling Stone* magazine's Robert Greenfield asked if the band were going to work on the new album at Keith's house, Richards replied, "Yeah, right in me own basement, as it turns out. After months of searching I end up sitting on it." The situation at Nellcôte grew partly from the fact that nobody found a suitable studio, but increasingly from a growing realization that the band would have to work around Keith's availability.

The years 1971–72 were undoubtedly when the public became aware of Keith's role at the heart of the band. With a front man as visual as Jagger—and a personality as strong—it's not surprising that most people considered him the kingpin. For many years, Keith was content with this state of affairs; it suited his role as a man of few words, a man of action, and allowed him to get on with what he was good at.

Keith Richards with National steel guitar, 1972 US tour.
(PHOTO: JOE SIA, STAR FILE)

Yet as far back as the mid-1960s, the businessmen knew where the real impetus came from. When Allen Klein made his move in 1965, the whole Stones team were seated around a table at the Scotch of St. James Club. Klein asked Andrew Oldham, "Which one makes the records?" Oldham pointed at Keith and said, "That one."

By 1971, the prospect of sitting around some studio in Nice, day and night, waiting for Keith to turn up would have been unthinkable—impractical, illogical, and a damned long waste of time and money. At Nellcôte, Keith worked when he wanted to, regardless of who was present and who was not—if Jagger, or Wyman, or the whole band were absent, it made little difference. For a songwriter who worked so much by *feel,* a home studio was the perfect situation. Once the basement was rigged up and £65,000 of recording equipment parked outside in the Rolling Stones Mobile, there was always somebody on hand to roll the tapes. Keith could work as the spirit moved him.

So, notwithstanding the scale of the project, this really is Keith's record from start to finish. You can feel it. Not a solo album, not a Keith Richards Production. With his simple, structural guitar (or piano) parts grounding every track, his presence pervades *Exile* more than any Stones album before or since, more even than on his solo albums.

The third key has to do with nationality. *Exile* was the last album the Stones made as Englishmen. Perhaps because their sense of nationality was heightened by French surroundings, the record has a determinedly English rock feel to it. This quality would subsequently vanish from later albums, as the band joined that élite troupe of wealthy world citizens: pleasure-seeking cosmopolitans of indeterminate and largely irrelevant national origins. Jagger and Richards arrived at this status well before the other band members, on the strength of their joint songwriting royalties. However, professional management, astute investment advice, and a chain of interlocking companies—effectively subcontracting the band to make records and appear in concert—minimized taxes and made everyone wealthy within a few years of Klein's eventual departure.

Even after long residence in America, a side of Keith will always remain a sausage-egg-and-chips Englishman, a Good Bloke, albeit one with dual nationality and all the resources that enormous wealth and status confer whenever needed—and nothing much could change Charlie Watts. But the Mick Jagger of the 1990s is surely an Americanized member of the supranational super-rich, and has been since the middle to late 1970s. Floreat Studio 54.

The more Mick struggles to demonstrate Englishness, on such media occasions as call for it, the more its essence appears to elude him. Those effortless modulations which were so much part of his 1960s persona—well-spoken, earnest young gent into "gor-blimey guv" Cockney—are pure English schoolboy humor, and they also had the feel of a joke shared with the other Londoners in the band. The bewildering array of personae on display these days are just as well executed, but much less satisfying. Too often, they are parodies of parody—somewhere along the line the cardinal points of the personality have drifted out of alignment.

Nobody can know the inner man, although his friend Keith has said:

I love Mick. Most of my efforts with Mick go to trying to open his eyes: "You don't need to do this. You have no problem, all you need to do is just grow up with it." Mick should stop trying to be Peter Pan. I don't see the point of trying to be 25 when you're not—he's obsessed with his age.

This question of Englishness may seem irrelevant to a band performing American music, but their versions of the American classics—and the Jagger/Richards songs inspired by them—were always filtered through a particularly English sensibility. That dynamic which, in every genre of popular music, has kicked ideas back and forth across the Atlantic for the better part of this century gets muddied and diluted when it becomes *too* knowing. Leave multinational corporate status to the record companies; they're the ones who deal in marketplace realities. The forces that made the young Stones inexorable were imagination, sex, an evangelical belief in the blues, coupled with an ability to turn on audiences of both sexes.

The gang who moved out of England in April 1971 had never really lived anywhere else for any period of time and for all their success were essentially still typical young Englishmen. Moreover, if we consider their teen and preteen years, they were English boys who'd grown up in what is now widely considered to have been a halcyon period for English youth. The headmaster of the primary school attended by Mick and Keith described a mid-1950s picture of the lads (reproduced in Philip Norman's book *The Stones*) as "English schoolboys at their apotheosis." Even when that was published in 1984, the opinion could have been considered an individual's nostalgia, but today it's a widely shared view of English life in the fifteen years following World War II.

Part of that postwar English scene was a largely imaginary, deeply rooted, and extremely innocent belief in America as a land of enchantment. The boys who became the Stones didn't make great records because of English music-hall songs or singalongs shared around the campfire. They began with a mission, a belief in the blues that bordered on the mystical and thrived on its distance and rarity. This belief, coupled with a parallel streak of healthy native skepticism, was enough to carry them into the 1970s. But once they had to leave France at the end of 1971, they drifted around the world, growing further apart from one another, and more out of touch with the attitudes, sense of humor, and experiences of the stock from which they had come. Exiles.

The majority of the basic tracks for *Exile on Main St.* were recorded at Nellcôte between July and November 1971. Then the master tapes were flown to Los Angeles, where American musicians (credited track by track in the sleeve notes) added overdubs at Sunset Sound and Wally Heider Studios. The sessions resumed at Sunset Sound after Christmas, and the lengthy process of mixing such a large number of songs with so many complex arrangements ran clear through until the end of March 1972.

In 1972 there were no compact disks, of course, only long-playing records, which consisted of two sides, each of which ran for about twenty-five minutes—much longer and you started to lose the bass response. *Exile* was conceived and executed as a double album with four discrete sides, not as a CD with eighteen consecutive tracks. Each side was a separate entity with its own internal dynamics. In the days of vinyl it was customary to open a side with a fast, catchy track and to close a side with the most powerful number available. In a world where people "auditioned" new LPs in a listening booth at the local record store, the decision whether to buy or not might well rest on the opening song. Closing a side with a punch meant the home listener was more likely to turn the album over than reach for a different record.

Exile's original four sides were:

1	2	3	4
Rocks Off	Sweet Virginia	Happy	All Down the Line
Rip This Joint	Torn and Frayed	Turd on the Run	Stop Breaking Down
Hip Shake	Black Angel	Ventilator Blues	Shine a Light
Casino Boogie	Loving Cup	I Just Want to See His Face	Soul Survivor
Tumbling Dice		Let It Loose	

Side One

Rocks Off Appropriately, for an album that is so much Keith Richards's conception, *Exile on Main St.* kicks off with the sound of Keith's solo rhythm guitar, chopping out one of his patent open-tuned intros. This leads in a strong up-tempo rocker that barrels along in time-honored Stones fashion. On many Stones albums it would be a stand-out track, but *Exile* contains moments of such clarity and candor that "Rocks Off" is overshadowed. However, that's a judgment that only comes with time and familiarity. The track is best regarded as an excellent attention grabber and momentum builder. It's well placed. To lead with one of *Exile's* subtler moments would be folly.

Just as the music of Charlie Parker, Miles Davis, and John Coltrane always retained a link to the simple verities of the blues (sometimes blindingly obvious, sometimes covert), there's a school of thought that holds that the further rock strays from its four grandparents—the simple, communal forms of the blues, the flash and excitement of 1950s rock 'n' roll, the dirt truths of muscular country music, and the church tradition of gospel—the weaker it gets.

Exile represents a mature synthesis of these American musics, filtered through a very English sensibility. What emerges is the finest flowering of original songs to come out of the whole blues-based English hard-rock scene (quite a different thing from heavy metal), a double album's worth of the highest-class rock.

Earlier in their career, the band made a good job of mixing a couple of these disparate elements to devise hit singles—for example, the three singles leading up to "Satisfaction." (I'm following the English releases, because they represent the Stones' own choices rather than those of their American record company.)

Consider "It's All Over Now" as a Merle Travis take on a Sam Cooke/Bobby Womack soul styling, followed up with a faithful rendition of "Little Red Rooster"—a single that introduced Willie Dixon and Howling Wolf to the *Billboard* pop chart in a country that had scarcely heard of them—their home country. Next came "The Last Time," a pure slice of Staples Singers gospel taken out of church and given a pre–heavy metal riff, a high, Everlys-style harmony vocal, and a superb, imaginative lead vocal.

Key words that always appear wherever *Exile* is analyzed are *dense, impenetrable,* and *crowded*—understandable, given the size and scope of the record, but really rather superficial impressions that collapse in the face of any detailed scrutiny.

Listen to "Rocks Off" on headphones and you can hear how carefully it's constructed. There's no "forest of guitars"—just Keith and Mick Taylor, bonding every bit as effectively as the original twin guitars of Richards and Brian Jones.

The first twelve seconds before the vocal enters should be enough to show that this is an arrangement that has been *thought about,* and constructed with considerable lucidity. If you bother to listen properly, it's anything but crowded—perfectly penetrable and as clear as the Aegean.

Keith's two-bar intro appears on the left, solo. A second guitar (almost certainly Mick Taylor) enters on the right, as Jagger manages to make a simple "oh yeah" sound thoroughly lascivious. At the center of the stereo image, the intro has a third element—either an organ or a guitar processed to sound rather like one—entering at the same time as Taylor, who plays a chugging, eight-to-the-bar pattern that opens out into chords. The "organ" plays a harmony to Keith's guitar, matching his phrasing beat for beat.

A characteristically effortless fill from Charlie brings in the band and we're off. Check the instrumentation in the opening verse and you'll find Keith slashing chords to the left, while on the other side a very clean-toned Mick Taylor plays a mixture of chords and connecting runs.

Nicky Hopkins's piano joins at the second part of the verse ("What's the matter with the boy?") placed in the center of the mix. As ever, he flows seamlessly from one style to another, sometimes vamping barrelhouse, at other times exchanging liquid, single-note runs with Mick Taylor; sometimes voicing octaves in the right hand, occasionally hammering rock 'n' roll eighth notes to build the final verse and chorus, and once, at 1:51, developing an extraordinary two-note idea for a couple of seconds before sweeping on. As with Bill Wyman's bass on this track, it's easy to overlook what a fine job is being done behind the main action.

The horns are held back, not appearing until they herald the first chorus, after which they expand into the mainstream. Here we have the sound of the basic five-piece rock band augmented by horns and the tastiest English rock pianist of the century; the full Rolling Stones rock combo as evolved on the road—a modern swing band.

After the second chorus comes a complete change of mood, at 2:11. In arrangement terms, this is the classic place for a bridge, but instead we get a breakdown. The song goes into half-time and the key modulates to the relative minor (an excellent way to produce a "spacey" effect). The bright, four-square sound of E major is exchanged for the distant, haunted, tonality of C-sharp minor.

As an evocation of a dislocated inner landscape, "get so mesmerized, all that inside," it's most effective—but 15 seconds' introspection is quite sufficient for a Rolling Stones track. No need to get *morbid*. Charlie kicks the band back into the fray and it's full speed ahead to the fade.

You have to strain to discern the lyrics, but nothing is spoiled on this account. For decades I heard the lines at 1:33 as "plug in flush out and fried my fuckin' feet." Huh? Not possible. Ultimately I prefer not to know.

Since the earliest days of rock, trying to understand the obscure phonetics and indecipherable lyrics of wild men like Little Richard and Jerry Lee Lewis has helped develop songwriters from Dylan to John Lennon. Whether the original lyrics gloss over inadmissible sexual innuendo, are the product of regional dialect, or simply cover up the fact that the composer hadn't finished the lyric doesn't matter a hoot. Making up your own sounds has always been part of the fun. Living proof of Fats Domino's adage that "you should never sing the words out very clearly."

Rip This Joint   Two bars of plain guitar, two cracks from Charlie's snare, and with a cymbal crash the band is straight in on the downbeat, rocking double-time. The brief snare fills at 7 and 12 seconds tell you at once that Charlie is *swinging*. Bill Plummer's upright walking-bass assists Charlie's case in a way that electric bass never could, even though it was over-dubbed half a world away.

Beneath the waterline, the track rests on three elements: bass, drums, and Nicky Hopkins's piano, where he pulls off one of his best party tricks. His playing is busy as hell yet never intrudes by so much as an inch. Same stunt he pulled off par excellence on the Who's "Anyway Anyhow Anywhere" single.

Those who complain that *Exile*'s sound is "murky" should try playing this track on the tiniest available speaker. Jagger's voice is perfectly clear, right at the front of the mix, with Charlie's backbeat keeping you snap on the offbeat. During the solos, you'd have to be deaf or seriously distracted to miss Bobby Keys's tenor sax. The piano is pretty far back, but it's clear enough during both of Keys's blistering horn solos. What more do you want? This is a prime AM radio mix.

Now go to the other extreme and put on the headphones. Myriad subtleties emerge. The last remastering for CD has certainly done a good job, but with headphones you'll hear just as well off the vinyl. Try it.

This is probably as close to the 1950s as the Stones had ever ventured in 1972. Here we have Keith's influence once again. Jagger sings up a storm—this is one great vocal—but his own tastes would have drawn him more to the new Stevie Wonder album than back to the 1950s. Artifacts from this recurrent urge to stay in step with the latest fashion can be found at every stage of the band's career, from those weak Marvin Gaye and Smokey Robinson covers on the early Stones albums through to the disco-era "Miss You."

Keith loves the rock 'n' roll he grew up with, as you hear on this track. Of all the 1950s rockers who influenced his generation of musicians, the strongest influence is not the most obvious. Paul McCartney, John Lennon, Clapton, and Keith himself have all testified to the personal influence of Buddy Holly. He wrote his own songs, which covered the full range of emotions, yet he built them out of the same simple, root-position chords that every beginner knows. With just a drummer and a stand-up bass he rocked as hard as a big band.

Little Richard and Elvis were exotics, creatures so alien they stood outside everyday life, but Buddy Holly was clearly a mortal. He wore glasses. He appeared at the London Palladium. And he revealed a Great

Truth: anyone who knew three chords could pick up a guitar and have a try. It could be done.

Jagger turns in one of his least restrained rock 'n' roll vocal performances here, a complete contrast with the lazy insouciance of "Rocks Off." A straight shouter that's interesting to consider alongside Lennon's "Twist and Shout." Mick continues to attract so much attention as an outfront showman that his best vocal performances tend to get overlooked. There are plenty of them, too, going right back to "Not Fade Away" and "The Last Time."

Jagger often derides his own early vocals, though he never doubted his ability to cover vocal inadequacy with *performance*. It's an odd fact that, despite his doubts, he almost always records "dry" (i.e., without artificial reverb or echo added to his vocal), while John Lennon, who possessed one of the great English rock voices, was plagued with doubt and constantly looked for new effects to alter the natural sound of his voice.

Though one outtake of this song has Keith "Ripping the Joint" on lead vocal, Jagger sings the final version, and between them, they work up a good witty lyric; a lubricious update of "Route 66," listing the attractions of various American cities, from San Jose down to Santa Fe, via Tampa, Memphis, Buffalo, Little Rock, New Orleans, Dallas, Birmingham Alabam', and even 'ole D.C.—where Dick and Pat (Nixon) are "gonna hold some shit for me." How much things would change in the six years that separate this from "Respectable" (1978); Jesse James with a "Get out of Jail Free" card.

As a maker of records (rather than a star guitarist) Keith is ably assisted, musically and morally, by the presence of Bobby Keys on tenor and baritone saxes. Most lead guitarist/composers would have taken at least one of the solos themselves, but tenor sax is far more appropriate in this context. A man of formidable appetites, Keys's tone on tenor sax is pure rabble-rousing Texas honk, and his very presence forms a direct line through to the 1950s rockers. Keys also lays down some fine baritone sax, low down in the mix. Its role in the arrangement is that of a musical carpet. In today's recording world, a similar role would be served by synth "string pads." Mixed correctly, a good pad provides a warm, rich layer that smoothes the sound, fills any holes, and sounds wonderful on the radio. It will also cover a weak vocal or a mediocre composition.

Keys was born on the same day as Keith, and the two formed an immediate bond, when they met on the Stones' first U.S. tour. The tour opened in San Bernardino, California, and the bill was loaded with the inevitable singing Bobbys: Vee, Goldsboro, and Comstock. The second stop was one of those mixed-media affairs that were a fixture of American life, but must have seemed surreal beyond belief to the Englishmen. At the Texas State Fair in San Antonio, the Bobbys and the Stones played two nights on a bill that included rodeo riding, trampolinists, and a menagerie of elephants and performing chimpanzees, before the night was topped off by the great George Jones.

Keys was enchanted by the Stones' slovenly appeal and casual onstage profanity (they would not have realized the extent to which American ears were protected against everyday workingman's language), and a friendship took root and developed over decades. Not only did he share a birthday with Richards, they were both used to being the youngest members of their respective bands. Keys was a natural hell-raiser (of a somewhat cruder stamp than Keith, but that's Texas for you), and a shared love of the same music—and later of the same drugs—sealed the friendship.

Those who imagine that poor suffering musicians are driven to drugs by the rigors of endless touring are laboring under a rather romantic delusion. What young man in his twenties would choose to work eight hours a day in a factory or dig roads if the alternative is running around America—in an old van or luxury jet—pursued by women, and getting paid for the privilege? The truth is that musicians take drugs because they *like* them. And if they take a lot of drugs, it's because they like them very much.

"Rip This Joint" is a celebration of Americana, especially the American South of Little Richard, Jerry Lee, and others. It's closer to the English Pop Art vision of a mythic United States—land of pink Cadillacs and white-wall tires—than to the muted photorealism of Robert Frank's collection *The Americans* (1959), with its prairie-flat, expressionless faces and solitary barroom jukeboxes, which appear on the cover of *Exile on Main St.*

Hip Shake   Or "Shake Your Hips," if you'd rather. A tribute to one of the greats:

> Well I met this girl / In a country town
> She said whaddya know / There's Slim Harpo

James Moore, a.k.a. Slim Harpo, to whom the Stones most properly give the due composing credit (unlike some of the blues-rock behemoths

Cool, calm, collected. An unruffled Charlie Watts at the LA Forum, June 11, 1972. (PHOTO: CORBIS/NEAL PRESTON)

of the day). No talk here of sponsoring a "Blues Museum" with the profits from stolen songs.

Keith sets the track rolling, not with one of his blockbuster intros but with the plain Slim Harpo/John Lee Hooker guitar boogie phrase, gateway to some of the finest blues (and some of the dullest blues-rock) imaginable. This one grooves. After a couple of times around, he's joined by Charlie. Listen hard at 0:11, following the entry of Bill Wyman's bass, for a brief, minor-key guitar phrase, replying to the main riff—Mick Taylor's entry.

With the groove set, Jagger starts singing in a stylized voice that's unique to this track. A dab of very short, very fast repeat echo adds an appropriately 1940s–1950s sound to the voice and creates an aural image of the sort of low, tin-roofed jukejoints where the original version was sung. Jagger's vocal grows more mannered, his vibrato more accentuated, as the song proceeds.

The critics divided. All agreed it was an outrageous piece of posturing, but some liked it, some didn't. In *Rolling Stone,* Lenny Kaye thought it "fine," while *Melody Maker*'s Richard Williams thought it constituted Jagger's sole lapse on the album—his voice "maintains the kind of taut authority which he hasn't always commanded, slipping into unnecessary affectation only on 'Hip Shake.'"

New track, new persona. Jagger's performance here makes the track unforgettable. If you're in any doubt, compare the earlier take available on various boots. The instrumental track isn't as polished, but that makes no real difference. Jagger sings the same lyric but in a much straighter tone, no mannerisms, no affectations—no *performance.* The take never really lifts off the ground. A singer has got to live up to his song. He can easily fall short; at best he can transcend it. The finished track on *Exile* owes a great deal to Jagger's inventiveness. His blues-harp is played with equal alacrity. The chorus features Bobby Keys's horn replying to Jagger's vocal; the outro features Jagger's harp exchanging phrases with the horns.

Charlie Watts, whose heart clearly has a home in the "wide-open" Kansas City of the late 1930s, beats out a rickety-tick pattern throughout on a drum hoop rather than drum-skin. Every so often he gives the proceedings a kick with a well-timed rim-shot on the snare, in time-honored vaudeville tradition. The first of these appears at 0:55, and the device is all the more effective for its sparing use.

Compare Keith Moon in the Stones *Rock 'n' Roll Circus.* The Who are in top form and the Stones, effectively a four-piece having to carry Brian Jones, are no match. During the clippity-clop "come on old hoss" segment of Townshend's "A Quick One," Moon upends one of his floor toms, rests it sideways atop his snare, and plays a very similar type of rhythm on the drum's metal shell. Needless to say, as the song segues into its next section, Moon sends the redundant tom flying off, stage left.

Among other problems (and there were plenty) the Stones' performance at their *Rock 'n' Roll Circus* was clearly not relaxed. "Hip Shake" is a different matter. The track simultaneously moves *and* stays loose as a goose. That effortless quality that is natural to so much black music sounds so easy—yet it defeats most rockers who try it.

Surprisingly, perhaps, "Hip Shake" never saw action in the live set.

Casino Boogie   Side 1 maintains the standard with another excellent song, a mid-tempo shuffle that slips straight into a groove and holds it all the way to the end.

Keith lays down a fine guitar figure in the left channel, and almost immediately Mick Taylor slides in on the opposite side. In under ten seconds the pair have a push-pull figure going, which gives the track its dynamic. The two guitars are supplemented by some preliminary pumpings from Keith Richards's bass guitar.

There's also something going on between the 4- and 6-second marks; something compressed and fuzzy happening low down. A sound from an unidentified instrument, probably a fuzz-bass, possibly an overdriven baritone sax or Mellotron? It swells and then it's gone. Such a tiny touch, but evidence of the attention to detail that characterizes the album.

Jagger's vocal enters and the percussion keeps time, the whole first verse being carried without any drums. Listen to Keith's bass phrase that accompanies the chord change up to D (0:24)—inspired. Similar phrases appear throughout the track.

Equally rocking is Charlie's opening drum fill, which kicks in the second verse. It's not only a great, explosive fill, it's wonderfully recorded. The relevance of Jimmy Miller's own background as a drummer becomes clear when you listen to the sound he gets on Charlie's kit. Prior to "Honky Tonk Women" the Stones drum sound was never like this. Or as high in the mix . . .

The heat of the Riviera summer played havoc with the guitars, which would frequently drift out of tune in the course of a three-minute recording, but it also affected the drum-skins. Jimmy Miller recalls:

It was midsummer on the Riviera when we cut most tracks. It was very humid and very hot working in the basement where we recorded. It was hard keeping the guitars in tune, and it was often difficult to get a really good drum sound. We spent a lot of time getting together little things.

The lyric is Jagger at his most fragmented. As Lenny Kaye pointed out:

[Since] Jagger's voice has been dropped to the level of just another instrument, burying him even more than usual, he has been freed from any restrictions the lyrics might have once imposed. The ulterior motives of mumbling aside, with much of the record completely unintelligible—though the words I could make out generally whetted my appetite to hear more—he's been left with something akin to pure singing, utilizing only his uncanny sense of style to carry him home.

This is spot on. With the narrative element excised, he rambles through the verses, sometimes double-tracking a high harmony part, intoning a mixture of random images, some pretty much gibberish, others elliptical fragments of Riviera life with some very funny lines: "Dietrich movies, close up boogies / Kissing cunt in Cannes."

Oddly, Lenny's critique then veers off course, suggesting that "'Casino Boogie' sounds at times as if it were a Seventies remake from the chord progression of 'Spider and the Fly' and for what it's worth, I suppose I'd rather listen to 'jump right ahead in my web' any day."

This is a bit wide of the mark. Such similarity as does exist between the two tracks is *rhythmic:* the chord progressions are quite different. "Spider and the Fly" is a strict 12-bar, while "Casino Boogie" changes chord where and when the melody dictates. If a reviewer is going to get technical, it's often considered an advantage to be accurate. Ultimately none of that matters a hoot if you *enjoy* the track, and it seems to me a first-class hunk of rock.

The first solo is taken by Bobby Keys, and there's just time for a catchy final verse, "Left foot shuffle, right foot muffle," before Mick Taylor's guitar takes over the lead and runs to the fade. The first eight bars feature a single guitar, then as Charlie opens the track out onto the ride cymbal, Taylor starts duetting with himself, playing the blues against sparse bottleneck lines. At 2:50, Nicky Hopkins hammers out a short burst of piano triplets, which Keith's bass immediately picks up and answers with an ascending run, bubbling up from depths.

With Jagger's remarks about *Exile* being a "dance record" in mind, one wonders just what it is that makes people want to dance. Nowadays there's a special chart solely for Dance Music (and its contents don't sound much like this), but if dance music is taken in a broader sense I'd define it as any music to which you can't keep still. This is dance music.

Tumbling Dice   Sublime. It's songs like this that the Stones were put on Earth for. Hard rock with swing and heart; gospel true and sleazy, too; *maestoso.* Must have been a brute to mix. So many fine ingredients—how to place them all without disturbing the equilibrium?

Analysis is largely superfluous when the target is hit this cleanly, although we know from various outtakes how much hard work went into achieving the final form. The song had a long gestation period, knocking around in rough form for a couple years before it was finally nailed.

Under the working title "Good Time Women," it first appears among a batch of songs from the early *Sticky Fingers* sessions of March 1970. In this form, the beautiful sliding guitar intro is absent, although the related guitar figure that underlies "You got to roll me" on the finished version is there, complete and intact in the key of G.

Add water and stir. Mick Jagger in Holland, 1973. (Photo: Laurens van Houten, Star File)

THE ROLLING STONES: EXILE ON MAIN ST.

The most interesting difference is tempo. "Good Time Women" rocks along at 120 beats per minute—fully 10 beats per minute faster than its counterpart on *Exile.* The most telling difference is the coda. The majestic climax on *Exile* is achieved by holding down a rock-solid tempo as the level of excitement builds. No matter how many new ingredients are flung into the mix, the tempo doesn't budge an inch. Charlie has it nailed. By contrast, the same section of the demo runs away with itself. It just keeps on speeding up until it's reached 130 beats per minute by the fade—a massive acceleration by any standards.

Apparently small differences in tempo—as little as 2 or 3 beats per minute—make all the difference to the feel of a song. With a good drummer you know at once when you've found the right tempo, because everything sits right. "Tumbling Dice" is one of the songs that causes occasional onstage rows between Mick and Keith, Mick wanting to push the tempo and Keith trying to hold it back on the "sweet spot."

The old Stax/Volt touring troupe used a simple tactic to add excitement to their live shows, clearly evident when you watch archive footage of Otis or Sam and Dave—"Don't dawdle between numbers, and play everything at twice the written speed." For raw excitement it can't be beat, and it's a sure-fire method for getting a crowd going, but it sacrifices a certain amount in the way of feel. There are moments when you can hear the horn section struggling heroically to fit in their written parts, but at such high tempos, the lines just can't be articulated.

On the album, "Tumbling Dice" is taken at exactly the right tempo—just a notch below 110 beats per minute—to allow the song to breathe. From Keith's single bar intro to the closing peak of the coda, Charlie holds the tempo right on the spot.

The descending, open-tuned lead-in gets my vote as Keith Richards's finest intro. There's the sound of the 5-string, open-G tuned guitar (capoed at the fourth fret to move the song into the key of B). The ringing open strings produce a tone that can't be found in standard tuning. Then there's the way the intro is voiced. The suspended chords produce a sense of tension waiting to be resolved. You're left up in the air until the chords resolve to a simple major with the entrance of the full band. All achieved in a single bar!

Not that you need to understand theory to feel the full force of the music; any more than Keith would have written it from a technical standpoint. An instinctive musician, an ear player, his normal method is to sit and chip away at a riff until it feels right to him. I've watched him stalk a single four-bar progression for several hours, around and around the loop, gradually locking onto the chords I was playing, then equally slowly, changing them; a note here, an accent there, until the emphasis shifted and the ghost of a "Stones feel" was present. It's a method unique in my experience, one in which the passage of time plays no part whatever.

Don't imagine that lack of theoretical knowledge translates into simplistic writing. Both "Can't You Hear Me Knocking" and "Live with Me" have exquisite, complex passages, but they're so natural sounding they don't strike you as anything especially tricky. Though he'd never admit it, Keith doesn't know the names of many of the chords he plays—they're just *shapes* in the song. He's a highly accomplished "songwriter" guitarist, the polar opposite of those showy, technique-driven lead guitarists who use speed and flash to create an impression and dazzle the credulous.

Amid the diversity of fans gathered by the Stones in a career approaching its fortieth year, I still find "Tumbling Dice" works as a litmus test. You can sort out a particular type of Stones fan by the status they accord this song. Some think it definitive, others can't see what the fuss is about.

The rough version, "Good Time Women," had a pretty undistinguished set of lyrics, though they scanned much the same and fitted the changes in a similar manner. Speaking to Roy Carr of *New Musical Express,* Jagger said, "Keith had some words to that one which we used when cutting the backing track. Then after a while we looked at each other and said: 'I don't like that.' So I went away and wrote those lyrics about gambling."

Somewhere in the mix, Mick Jagger's credited with one of the guitars, but it's impossible to pick out—if it's there at all. Fortunately, the rewritten lyrics, which are some of Jagger's best, *can* be picked out—most of them, anyway. Even when their sense is not always distinguishable, their sound and rhythm are still an essential part of the song. And that's all right with me. Death to lyric sheets!

When asked in *Melody Maker* about the low vocal, Jagger replied, "I think they used the wrong mix for that one. I'm sure they did," though by all accounts the final weeks mixing at Sunset Sound turned into something of a nightmare. Jagger told Roy Carr:

Mixing, things just seemed to go on and on. Getting it finished got to be really drawn out towards the end. I suppose it was just 'cause it was a lot of songs . . . double album. It was the last bit, you know? Getting all the sound mixes right. After you've been working on it for so long, that last bit has got to be perfect.

Exile is the album on which the Stones perfected the art of the extended, rolling coda—the slow deliberate build to a climax, with the gradual introduction of new elements. The device is used so well on *Exile* we are spoiled for choice—both "Torn and Frayed" and "Tumbling Dice" are fine examples—though the most powerful by far (and the longest) is found at the end of "Tumbling Dice."

In a track lasting 3:45, fully 1:24 is taken up by the coda, leaving a basic verse-chorus, verse-chorus song of just 2:21. A brief preview of the coda occurs just before the guitar solo—which I take to be Keith, as it rings the same set of changes on a simple theme as the "Gimme Shelter" solo. Neither break is likely to gather much praise from jazz-rock purists or technique freaks, but for those who like a simple statement expressed with maximum economy, these are two solos to be venerated. "Tumbling Dice" *may* be a composite solo—a cut-and-paste job. Two-thirds of it is plainly in Keith's Chuck Berry style, but there's a possible edit at 2:02, where the tone changes slightly. An overdub? Two guitar parts cross-faded? Whichever, the closing phrases build the solo to a satisfying close, bringing us that much nearer to the coda.

So how is the "Tumbling Dice" coda built? Simply. Deceptively simply.

A pair of headphones will reveal a lot. The foundation (as always) is Keith's rhythm guitar, which states a basic descending phrase. This two-bar loop keeps on running beneath everything. As each new element joins, it too keeps on going, rolling until the fade, so that the arrangement resembles a horizontal stack, growing taller.

The choir, led by Jagger, sings "You got to roll me" from the first bar. Jagger dodges to and fro, sometimes with the choir, sometimes answering them. At 2:29, the chords are thickened by Mick Taylor's bass (one note for each chord) and Nicky Hopkins's piano, which plays "spread" (lightly arpeggiated) chords in unison with the bass.

Next time around, a second guitar joins in, thickening the sound by playing unison with the first. After a single loop it's joined by a baritone sax playing a classic soul-band figure—three notes down, three notes up. The best place to hear this is around 2:40—also the point at which the bass breaks out from single notes and starts moving.

At 2:46, Charlie, who until now has restricted himself to the occasional accent here and there, starts an insistent beat on the toms: a Red Indian, "Kawliga," or Glitter Band beat, according to your cultural reference point. Then at 2:53, the choir's call of "You got to roll me" draws a response—"Keep on rollin'." Just past the 3:00 mark, Charlie breaks out of his measured pattern, onto the full kit. With a fill and a cymbal splash he finally releases the tension and sets the whole great edifice in motion, like a liner finally leaving the slipway and fully entering the water. The crescendo—the launch—is so deftly handled you could happily listen to a further two or three minutes, but on the principle of never giving away too much of a good thing, a slow fade begins and the vessel disappears over the horizon.

Side Two

> We ended up putting all the acoustic sounding things like "Sweet Virginia" and "Torn and Frayed" all on one side because they seemed to fall together.
>
> —KEITH RICHARDS, *NEW MUSICAL EXPRESS*

Sweet Virginia   Side two, the pastoral side of *Exile*—"the side you can play late at night or first thing in the morning"—opens with this mid-tempo country song. What better way to follow the high of "Tumbling Dice," where every instrument in the armory is employed, with the relaxed, back-porch sound of an acoustic guitar and Mick's harp? Such variety. At this point in time there wasn't a rock 'n' roll band within hailing distance of the Stones. For a brief moment, good taste shared common ground with the interests of commerce.

Keith's guitar playing had always suggested a degree of interest in country and western. From the cover of Hank Snow's "I'm Moving On" on *December's Children,* to the country inflections on "It's All Over Now" (which brought allegations from the English music press that "they'd gone country"), the influence was there. But it was the time spent with Gram Parsons, the ex-Byrd and Flying Burrito Brother, that really taught Keith Richards about country. Sitting at the piano, hammering out Hank Williams numbers with this Georgia-born native, gave Keith a chance to absorb the cadences of true country music; the inflections, the "tear" in the voice, all the little nuances that lift a song and reach out to the listener.

Country and Western did not enjoy a very good reputation with the underground of the 1960s. In England, the music was associated principally with rednecks, racism, and reaction. A movement centered on opposition to the war in Vietnam found little it could relate to in the patriotic ballads of Merle Haggard. When people did accidentally stumble across "accept-able" country—for example, Pennebaker's hotel room footage of Dylan busking Hank Williams's "Lost Highway" in the film *Don't Look Back* (Hank Williams's version is a straight rerun of the Ernest Tubb original)—they probably took it for a Woody Guthrie tune.

"Five strings, two fingers and one asshole."—Keith Richards (PHOTO: CORBIS/NEAL PRESTON)

The divisions within country music that distinguish cloying, overproduced Nashville schmaltz from the white man's blues of Ernest Tubb, Jimmie Rodgers, Hank Williams, Johnny Cash, George Jones, Merle Haggard, and others aren't always immediately apparent to Americans, let alone to Englishmen. Jagger never got it at all. It took the instincts of a "feel" player like Keith to distinguish the good from the mediocre. To anyone with an ear for that elusive, indefinable quality that makes a music "true," the distinction is quite clear; and the link between Elvis, Buddy Holly, Jerry Lee Lewis, and pure country is as clear as their link to the blues.

THE SONGS

Jagger's phobia of being thought "hokey" or out of touch has always manifested itself as a series of eager pounces on the fashionable mode. He seems to have been determined to keep up with the Latest Thing, wherever it led—no matter how well- or ill-suited it might be to the Stones' fairly limited skills as a band. They are, after all, a rock 'n' roll band, not an all-purpose showband, equally at home playing Top 40, Duke Ellington, or strict tempo.

Though Jagger could twist his voice and persona with remarkable flexibility, the one genre in which he consistently missed the mark was country. He seems to have felt compelled to play it for laughs—no bad thing in itself, except that he doesn't do it terribly well. Listen to "Dear Doctor" or "Far Away Eyes," where he selects ludicrous cracker-parody accents, often preferring to speak verses rather than sing. Embarrassment, I suspect. Sad, because he sounds good when he does sing it straight.

"Sweet Virginia" is sung with great feeling. It's not that he can't do it, more that he fears the mockery of his smart uptown buddies. If there's one American music that's anathema to the assiduous social climber, it's the voice of the trailer park, the sound of po' white trash. Unlike "Far Away Eyes," "Sweet Virginia" is sung "properly." It has a great lyric about the state of contemporary California, and a passing reference to Altamont, "Thank you for your sweet and bitter fruit." But, you can't help noticing that Jagger bites down on the word "shit" with a little more relish than is really necessary—as though schoolboy naughtiness will cover any accusations of hokiness.

"Sweet Virginia" was another song that had been in the can for some time. There are versions from 1969 and 1970, but presumably they were never finished or were put aside for later use. The most common alternate take in circulation is similar to the final version, notable only for a rather leaden I–V oom-pah bass, and Ian Stewart's prominent barrelhouse piano.

The deeper you delve into *Exile,* the greater your respect becomes for the concept, the attention to detail, and the plain record-making skills the band had developed in their ten years before the mast. Good 'ole "Sweet Virginia" is as cleverly put together and neatly developed as "Tumbling Dice." Let's look at the components.

The song opens with another of Keith's deceptively understated solo acoustic guitar intros, plain, yet articulated with the same rhythmic subtlety as "Torn and Frayed" or "Love in Vain." The song is in A major, but

Keith's acoustic guitar, which carries the track, is capoed at the second fret, shifting it into the ringing, guitar-friendly key of G major—much better for picking.

Jagger's blues-harp enters next, solo on the first line; shadowed thereafter by a guitar picked mandolin-style. After thirty seconds this guitar stops playing unison and throws in a couple of country inflected licks, before snaking off onto a switchback scale in triplet time (0:44 to 0:47), establishing a motif that reappears at key moments throughout the song.

Bass and drums sit out the intro, entering with Jagger's vocal at the start of verse 1.

Verse 2 is distinguished by the appearance of Ian Stewart's piano and Bobby Keys's honky-tonk sax. The first harmony vocals appear at the chorus, a big block of them singing along barroom style.

Keys takes a fine raucous tenor solo, joined by handclaps, then it's back to a double chorus. Spot anything different about these choruses? Whereas the first chorus is sung ensemble, these are performed in call and response gospel style, "COME ON—come on, COME ON DOWN—come on down." On a casual listening, one misses these details, but I think that's intended. The variations, the shifting instrumentation, the constant changing of small details work as subliminal hooks, demonstrations of Keith's adage, "Always introduce something new every ten seconds."

The songs ends with a classic country rallentando, or slowdown. The drums stop, a chord hangs in the air, and the voices stretch the final word over an extra chord. Anyone who's ever sung a hymn will recognize it as the plagal cadence (IV to I)—the two chords of the "A-men."

With its groove and its gospel-inflected backing vocals, this is music a thousand miles away from the million-selling, easy-listening California sound that would shortly become known as Country Rock. A successful amalgam of country, blues, and gospel, it is quintessential Rolling Stones, in fact.

A less imaginative arrangement would have given the solo to a pedal steel guitar—a more obviously "country" instrument—and not to Keys's godless, rasping horn. But the pedal steel is held over for the next track, the ballad "Torn and Frayed."

Torn and Frayed The Rolling Stones in excelsis. How can the guitar *not* steal your heart away? In another of those majestic fadeouts, Al Perkins's soaring pedal steel guitar leads the song up and into the sunset, slowly looping higher and higher, every instrument working together. Nicky Hopkins's piano and Jim Price's organ, Mick Taylor's wonderfully mobile bass lines swooping down, then leaping high into the treble register, freed from the conventional bass role by Charlie's drums and Keith's two immovable guitars, which form the rhythm section and take care of the foundations.

All this develops from a lone, standard-tuned acoustic guitar. Keith strumming simple root chords, D, A, then *working* that low E chord (start of the second bar, or the 0:03 mark) to get the most out of the lowest note on the guitar. Charlie completes the two-bar intro with a restrained fill and brings in piano, bass, and Jagger's vocal on the downbeat.

In the left channel, Keith comes straight in after the first line of vocal with one of those neat, balanced phrases that the Fender Telecaster was built for; a line that reappears in several different registers throughout the song—Robbie Robertson out of Curtis Mayfield. The rest of the time, the Telecaster plays simple chops on the off beat, beefing up the snare drum.

Stage center in the stereo image, Jagger's fine lead vocal is joined at key moments in the verses by Keith's high harmony vocal, leaning in from the right. In the choruses the lead vocal is buttressed on both sides, by several layers of tracked harmony; if you listen hard you can hear Keith stretching certain words with the country "swell" Gram Parsons taught him (listen for the words "seen" and "better" in the choruses).

A sense of balance runs through the whole arrangement. Instruments move around as the arrangement grows more complex, but the acoustic guitar always balances its mate, the electric guitar, while Nicky Hopkins's piano plays off Jim Price's organ (Jim enjoying a rare day off from his trumpet). The track has a feel reminiscent of The Band, circa Big Pink.

The free agent amidst all this balance is the steel guitar, which enters relatively late. Once it has the bit between its teeth, though, it completely runs away with the song, seizing the emotional high ground and growing increasingly poignant as it climbs the scale. A wonderful idea in arrangement terms, ideally fitted to the sense of the lyric—and a virtuoso performance by Al Perkins.

Built around a loose, semiautobiographical account of life on the road, the lyric uses the lead guitarist and his coat as metaphors, both for the Stones-at-large and for the redeeming power of rock 'n' roll at its best.

The two of them may be beaten up, torn, frayed, and they have definitely seen better days, but they fit one another, they're funky, and on a good night they still have the power to knock you clean off your feet—to steal your heart away. As a description of the hit-and-miss quality of the Stones live, and of the potency of the best music, it's a pretty good image.

There's little doubt as to the identity of the lead character. If we accept Anita's theory that Mick always really wanted to be Keith, it's a sort of double love song, Jagger addressing both the subject and the object of desire. The song was written at a time when Bianca Jagger was throwing away clothes she'd lent Anita rather than ever wearing them again—and when Keith's habits and general way of life reached their most beautiful expression in his appearance. Keith's funky, charismatic ragamuffin quality is nicely described. Despite this, any resemblance between the song's characters and persons living or dead should not be taken *too* literally.

"Joe" has a cough and requires codeine to fix it. With a willing doctor and a conscientious pharmacist, who's gonna help him to kick it? Codeine of course is one of the byproducts in the manufacture of heroin, but the word codeine has a nicer ring to it, as well as an historical background in folk-blues songs.

We somehow can't picture Keith shambling up to a pharmacy and requesting a "bottle of codeine linctus, please," in order to hold his habit at bay for a few hours, any more than we can imagine the entire band a "bag of nerves" on first nights—Ian Stewart, strong man of the group, collapsed and weeping in a corner, "I cannae do it, I cannae go through wi' it," while Jagger bites his nails and Mick Taylor nervously adds a third coat of blue eyeliner—yet the images serve.

Only the pictures of endless ballrooms and parasite-filled dressing rooms bear the unmistakable quality of having been drawn from life; and the payoff line, as every one of us knows, is a literal truth about the transcendent quality of the best live music. There's no accounting for it, the everyday numbers don't add up, but on a good night it *will* steal your heart away, sending you back out into the street a different person from the one who came in—for a while, anyway.

"Torn and Frayed" has some lovely moments of transition (verse to chorus or bridge to solo) where one or another instrument finds exactly the right phrase to mark the change: Jim Price's two-note organ fill at 0:53, linking verses 1 to 2; and Al Perkins's pedal steel at 1:43, connecting the chorus to the start of his solo proper. Hear Charlie open out the coda at 3:37, by switching from the closed sound of the high hat to the swish of the ride cymbal, and Al Perkins respond three seconds later as his steel guitar peels off, right at the ceiling of its range, into a slow four-note cascade.

Played on the opening night of the 1972 U.S. tour at Vancouver, the song was promptly dropped from the set for most of the tour and has never subsequently made much of a showing live. A point where one must take issue with the press—*Rolling Stone*'s review claims the track "has trouble getting started." This is alarming. One of the subtlest arrangements on the album, a finely crafted track that builds slowly, layer upon layer, to an achingly beautiful crescendo of guitars, steel guitars, girl backing singers, all from a single acoustic guitar? I know that Lenny Kaye plays guitar himself, and if this intro is in trouble, he should wish for a little of the same. True, he acknowledges the crescendo but fails to grasp that its origin lies in the smooth development from the simple solo guitar figure that opens the song.

Black Angel (or Sweet Black Angel)   A song written over an acoustic guitar groove, which sounds like something Keith had been kicking around for ages, waiting to find the proper setting. The marimbas (added later) create much of the Caribbean feel; the track could easily have taken a different direction. Let's be clear, as a basic track it's neither reggae nor calypso, just one of those circular figures that guitar players sometimes find themselves playing.

"Sweet Black Angel" did not start life as an anthem to the early 1970s favorite political pinup girl. It first shows up under the working title "Bent Green Needles," one of a dozen songs from the first *Sticky Fingers* sessions of March 1970—the first material recorded on the brand new sixteen-track mobile studio.

The new venue made no difference to the cast. Jimmy Miller was producing, and first engineer was Glyn Johns—the same Glyn Johns who'd sung with a group called the Presidents, shared a flat with Ian Stewart, and engineered the "Bright Lights, Big City" session by the (as yet) unsigned Stones at IBC Studios back in March, 1963. By 1970 Glyn's brother, Andy Johns, was assistant engineer, having graduated from tape operator at Olympic Studios in the *Satanic Majesties* days. Both worked on *Exile*.

"Black Angel" made a rare live appearance on the 1972 tour, in the afternoon show at Fort Worth, Texas, but didn't quite come off. The delicacy of the principal guitar part doesn't sit easily with the power rush of live performance—probably the groove is too precarious to risk hitting consistently, and the marimbas too essential to the sound. One of the many instruments Brian Jones played, they were his choice to give texture to "Under My Thumb" on *Aftermath*. The marimbas on "Sweet Black Angel" were overdubbed in L.A., by Richard "Didimus" Washington from Dr. John's band—who was so annoyed at the *Exile* sleeve crediting the work to "Amyl Nitrate" that he conjured a voodoo spell on the Stones. It was during these L.A. overdubs that the song's direction finally settled.

A monitor mix of the song, together with what Keith has said about the recording methods in France, give us a good idea of how this track was put together. The basic track (presumably from Nellcôte, because Anita describes it as one of the few songs that lured her down into the basement to dance) has Keith on acoustic guitars and Jimmy Miller on percussion. The bass guitar and mouth-harp *could* have been recorded at the same time, but I suspect not.

The first take would have recorded the main acoustic guitar (early on you can hear Keith humming snippets of the melody, as he feels his way into the guitar part) and Miller playing a "fish," or scraper, which keeps up a constant *chikka-chikka chikka-chikka* rhythm. In a second pass, Jimmy would have added the wood block, which plays variations on a *dut dut d-dut* beat, once every eight beats. Then Keith would have added the second acoustic guitar, which plays a delicate phrase, replying to the first guitar.

The track sounds to me as though it was built up as described, with bass guitar, Jagger's mouth-harp, and a guide vocal laid down at later sessions. From here there are a number of directions in which the song could have been developed.

The lyric, which concerns black activist Angela Davis, shows how wittily Jagger could write when he could be bothered. It stands at the opposite end of the spectrum to a lyric like "Silver Train"—a collection of Stones clichés that appear to have been assembled without any discernible mental activity. The Angela Davis case became a worldwide cause célèbre at a time when hostility towards Richard Nixon and support for the Black Panther Party could be more or less taken for granted among young people

in America and Western Europe—or at least among those likely to buy *Exile on Main St.*—a consensus unimaginable today.

Briefly, Angela Davis was the daughter of Alabama schoolteachers who became a doctoral candidate at the University of California, San Diego, under the Marxist professor Herbert Marcuse. In 1970, the California Board of Regents refused to renew her appointment as philosophy lecturer—despite an excellent record as an instructor on the L.A. campus— citing her "political opinions" as a reason. Championing the cause of black prisoners, Davis grew attached to one of the imprisoned Soledad Brothers, George Jackson. When an escape and kidnapping attempt at the Hall of Justice in Marin County went wrong (August 7, 1970), four people, including the judge, were murdered. Davis, who was suspected of complicity, went onto the F.B.I. "most wanted" list. Arrested in New York City in October 1970, she was returned to California to face charges of kidnapping, murder, and conspiracy.

In a double-tracked vocal, interspersed by his blues-harp and the marimbas, Jagger adopts a persona straight out of Uncle Remus—"Free de sweet black slave." Once again he pulls off a delicate balancing act, retaining the seriousness of subject while hamming it up like something out of a minstrel show. You can almost visualize the white gloves.

In one of its more deranged aesthetic judgments, the *Rolling Stone* review suggested the reggae singer Desmond Dekker as a model. What is interesting, amid the whole mass of reviews, is that nobody mentioned the phrase "protest song" or drew any parallels with Dylan. Either the press had grown up a little, or more likely, nobody noticed.

In early June, just as *Exile* hit the streets, an all-white jury acquitted Angela Davis of all charges.

Loving Cup   Another "old" song, "Loving Cup" was first recorded at Olympic during the June 1969 sessions that also produced versions of "All Down the Line," "Sweet Virginia," "Shine a Light," and "Stop Breaking Down." These sessions, which ran for most of the month, also served as an extended rehearsal for the new guitarist, Mick Taylor, who had joined the band in May. Of the songs that ended up as *Exile* tracks, only "Loving Cup" was included in the set of the free concert in Hyde Park, July 5, 1969—Taylor's live debut with the band.

From a collection of tapes that Jimmy Miller gave to friends of mine (which ended up on the auction block at Sotheby's) comes a wonderful six-and-a-half minute early version of "Loving Cup." The circulating copy is slightly overrecorded, but not enough to spoil the pleasure of hearing one of *Exile*'s memorable songs as a work in progress. Jagger has his part pretty well finalized, the only notable difference being a second, discarded bridge at 3:39, with lyrics about misty lakes and cold sunrises that don't quite match up to the rest. The released version ends with the repeated call, "Gimme little drink." The outtake will forever be known as the "Had a Little Drink" version, since Jagger rants and rages through the final 90 seconds with increasingly petulant and incoherent demands for a drink. Excellent method acting, or a hard night at the studio.

This outtake demonstrates that while some songs needed time to evolve, others in the stockpile were ready to go. From a songwriter's perspective, the differences between the two versions are not great. They amount to little more than some reshaping and a good polishing up: the musicians settling on their parts, and an editing down of the arrangement. The master take of "Loving Cup" must have been a breeze.

The Stones had become increasingly used to developing songs in the studio. The days of recording a completed arrangement in a single three- or six-hour session were long gone. The band would happily spend days at Olympic working up the germ of an idea, hunting around for a "feel," trying to lock onto a groove, and running up large studio bills.

Jimmy Miller tried to get them to do preproduction work at their warehouse/rehearsal space in Bermondsey, which had a four-track tape machine "but only Bill and Charlie showed up. The only way to get them all there was to book the studio proper and say, 'this is a session, you gotta show up, we're paying a hundred pounds an hour.'"

As one of the two leading bands on the planet, unlimited studio time was a luxury they considered theirs by right. But with a financial crisis looming as the relationship with Klein deteriorated, someone—probably Jagger—decided there was a more sensible option. Figuring that the money spent block-booking Trident or Olympic Studios could be better spent buying their own recording equipment, they fitted out a truck with a desk, a sixteen-track tape machine, and the usual outboard gear of the day—limiters, compressors, reverb plates, and so on. In addition to saving studio bills, the machine could earn its keep being hired out to other bands.

So in March 1970, the brand new Rolling Stones Mobile recording truck was parked outside Jagger's country seat, Stargroves, near Newbury in Berkshire, with huge, gaffer-taped bundles of cable running into the ground-floor rooms of the house, where the gear was set up. This way, the basic tracks could be recorded at leisure and the master reels then taken to Olympic for final mixing. Of the dozen or so tracks recorded at the sessions in March, 1970, "Tumbling Dice" (under its working title "Good Time Women") and "Bent Green Needles" were early versions of *Exile* songs. There's even an early version of "Waiting for a Friend," which didn't surface until the *Tattoo You* album in 1981.

The same method would be used for *Exile,* with the backing tracks from Nellcôte in their varying stages of completion, eventually being sweetened, overdubbed, and mixed in L.A.

Side 3

Happy   Keith's declaration of his personal philosophy, as it stood circa 1971. Should be borne in mind alongside his remark to *Rolling Stone* magazine's Robert Greenfield about Villa Nellcôte, "It's a pretty good house, we're doing our best to fill it up with kids and music."

At first the band commuted to Nellcôte from their own houses, which were dotted about the surrounding countryside, but clearly, this was never going to work. The Stones en masse were no more 9-to-5 men than they were midnight-to-6 men. Recording started—and halted—when Keith was in the mood. The only sensible option was for the band to come to him. Nellcôte became Stones Central (Vichy Desk) just as surely as Keith's hotel room became Divisional HQ when the band toured.

This suited some people better than others. "Imagine it. Thirty people for six months. I was so stressed out," said Anita, with considerable feeling. But it suited Keith, even if the arrangement sometimes made him the very public recipient of Anita's displeasure, she being in no doubt about the "music" but less certain that the most was being done to fill it with more kids.

Inevitably such a casual arrangement cut down the number of full-band sessions. Keith recorded as the mood took him, with whomever happened to be around, and the purest example of this method is "Happy," a spontaneous composition, knocked out in a single session at Nellcôte.

The seed of the song is the main guitar riff from the verse, which evidently grabbed Keith strongly enough to write the rest of the song around it, more or less at a sitting. Inspiration at work. A highly concentrated example of the songwriting method Keith has frequently expounded in interviews—namely, that you fish around for a while and hope to catch something.

It was high summertime and the fish were biting. Keith told Victor Bockris that the "basic track was Bobby Keys on baritone, myself on guitar, and Jimmy Miller on drums. 'Happy' was cut one afternoon. We were

basically doing the sound-check . . . and the track just popped out. It was just because, for a change, people weren't lying down on the beach or at a local bar in Nice. Sometimes I'd be ready to play and some guys would come over early."

Bobby Keys added percussion to Jimmy Miller's drums, Keith doubled the guitar part with a slide, added a bass guitar, then laid down a guide vocal. Basic track completed.

The song's construction is sufficiently simple, like a 1950s pop song, to allow such a lightning-fast recording. The verse is built around a single repeated phrase, just one bar long, and the chorus is a two-bar phrase with a single repeat. There's no bridge. About as simple a structure as you can get, it has the sound of a jam that has settled into place—or one of those rare songs that arrive fully formed, which the artist merely has to take down like dictation.

It's also a classic example of Keith's 5-string, open-G style. Open tuned guitars were nothing new around the Stones. As early as "I Wanna Be Your Man" (1963), Brian was playing Elmore James–style bottleneck in open-E tuning, and among his very last notes heard on a Stones record are the mournful, slide guitar cadences of "No Expectations" (*Beggars Banquet,* 1968). In fact the first time Mick and Keith laid eyes on Brian, at Alexis Korner's Ealing Club in early 1962, he was playing bottleneck under the name Elmo Lewis. A year older in age—but many more in experience—Brian seemed startlingly proficient to Mick and Keith.

Brian played standard, mainstream, open-E slide guitar (or open-D, same thing) in the style of Elmore James's "Dust My Broom," and simply adapted it to non-twelve-bar blues such as Lennon-McCartney's "I Wanna

Be Your Man." He did it so well that Keith doesn't seem to have played slide guitar or used open tunings at all while Brian was around. Keith's conversion came courtesy of Ry Cooder, who'd been brought in to play mandolin and guitar on the *Let It Bleed* sessions. Cooder used a different kind of open tuning, one associated less with electric Chicago blues and more with the older acoustic country blues, known as open-G.

The basic principle is very simple. The strings of a "normal" guitar are tuned randomly, such that the fingers of the left hand must be used to produce a major chord. As there are seven major chords (for the purposes of rock), a different hand shape must be learned for each chord. An open-tuned guitar is not tuned randomly. Every string is tuned to one of the three notes comprising the basic chord, so that the guitar can be struck without the use of the left hand and a major chord can be produced. To form other major chords, all the guitarist need do is place one finger across all the strings at a single fret. Different fret positions will produce different chords.

Of course there's more to it, but the basic proposition is that simple. It's common to see pictures of Keith, from 1969 onward, with his *left* hand in the air instead of holding down notes on the neck—the opposite of Pete Townshend, although they're both right handers. He's free to do this because once struck, his guitar is producing a G chord. The opening chords of "Honky Tonk Women" give you a perfect illustration of the simplest sound of open-G.

A guitar tuned to open-G can be hit with far greater vigor if the sixth string is taken off. Although Keith has had 5-string guitars custom built, over the years he's found that the instrument that answers best is the plain Fender Telecaster with the bridge slightly adapted and the sixth string-saddle removed. Four times out of five you'll find Keith using a Telecaster. In his own elegant phrase "Five strings, two fingers, and one asshole."

With the addition of two suspended chord shapes—the first is heard on the intro to "Brown Sugar," while *both* shapes can be heard on the intro of "Happy"—Keith had the tuning pared down to his needs. The sound of open-G became the definitive Rolling Stones sound, and that instantly recognizable, slashing, syncopated rhythm guitar style became Keith's trademark, a sound all his own. He didn't entirely abandon standard tuning or open-E, but open-G became the tuning of choice. As a very rough guide, one can say that as the 1960s ended, Keith moved from open-E ("Gimme Shelter") to open-G.

The first full-scale appearance of open tunings onstage was the Hyde Park free concert of July 1969. Preceding the days of electronic tuners, the event was the harmonic equivalent of Altamont—a nightmare of shifting capos and marathon tuning sessions had to be edited from the television footage. An heroically stoned Keith Richards appeared to have reached that stage of intoxication where even objects betrayed him—capos wouldn't snap shut, strings slipped off bridges, and pitch shifted treacherously, especially on the long, slender neck of the Gibson Flying V (surely the very worst instrument for the job). As a perfect cameo of that day, nothing betters the moment when, with the situation degenerating perilously close to farce, a nervous young Mick Taylor eventually crossed the stage—observed by giant images of a drunken Brian Jones laughing down at everybody—to tentatively offer Keith assistance getting the tuning back on an even keel. Anyone who's ever approached Keith on this type of mission, even in private, will understand Mick Taylor's reticence.

But in the studio, once he had absorbed Cooder's method (and if you read between the lines it's pretty clear that Keith is owning up to what is known as a "sponge job"), Keith developed what was essentially a rural American curiosity of the 1930s into a style suitable for 1970s commercial hard rock, capable of topping the pop singles charts. The list of songs that flow from Keith's discovery of this tuning is long, and effectively defines the Mark-2, post–Brian Jones, Rolling Stones. "Honky Tonk Women," "Brown Sugar," "You Can't Always Get What You Want," "Wild Horses" (which extends the tuning into minor-chord territory), "Can't You Hear Me Knocking," "Tumbling Dice"—and a majority of songs on *Exile,* including "Happy."

Turd on the Run   A steaming up-tempo rocker, "Turd" is built around a circular guitar riff that sounds familiar until you try and place it. Another fine vocal from Jagger, who also gets in on the instrumental action. His mouth-harp here is a real part of the structure, while on other tracks it's often primarily an embellishment.

Right on the 1:00 mark, a storming guitar enters the mix. It sounds like Taylor, but it's hard to tell (even for the people who played the parts). It holds its own for 35 seconds, so we must presume this is the solo, though it's evenly shared with Jagger's harp.

The track is propelled by a killer bass part. This is one of four tracks on the album to benefit from Bill Plummer's stand-up bass playing (the others being "All Down the Line," "I Just Want to See His Face," and "Rip This Joint"). For years, English fans wondered if he might not be a made-up character, along the lines of Amyl Nitrate (marimbas)—Bill Plummer, Plumber's Bill?—but no, he's just as real a person as Didimus, the real "Amyl Nitrate."

It's ironic that the player who adds walking bass lines to two of the rawest, most 1950s-sounding rock 'n' roll tracks on *Exile* is a distinguished jazz player. A career musician who majored in composition, harmony, and arranging at college, and studied under the principal bassist of the New York Philharmonic, Plummer's resume is impressive. He's played with Tony Bennett, Nancy Wilson, George Shearing, Lou Rawls, Miriam Makeba, Quincy Jones, Tom Waits, the Tommy Peltier Jazz Corps with Roland Kirk, and Miles Davis. In the session world, that's what you call a broad curriculum vitae.

How did he end up playing on *Exile?* Many of the musicians who graced the L.A. sessions in early 1972 were brought in courtesy of Dr. John, but Bill's route was different. He told me:

> I was collaborating with Wolfgang Melz and Jim Keltner on our two-bass project called *Basses International.* While sitting at home one evening, Jim Keltner called and said, "What are you doing tonight?" I said, "Just groovin', why?"
>
> Jim said, "How would you like to work with the Stones tonight?"
> My first thoughts were "Concert?"
> He said, "No, they want you to record string bass on a new album, four songs. Can you be down at Sunset Sound in, let's say an hour?"
> Of course I said yes.
> When I got there they had all the songs set up ready to go. It was the most organized professional recording I had worked on at that time. The fellows were all terrific and friendly. No craziness, no drugs. Joe Zagannao was the engineer. I played to the tracks to learn the songs, made a few notes on their charts, and all four songs went down with their choice of the first takes on all attempts.

I asked if anyone gave any direction or made suggestions. Or was it a case of just roll the tape, play along, then the familiar call of "yeah, great, come on in" from the control room? Bill replied:

> There were a few suggestions. But they seemed very happy with my feeling for the songs. Mick went over the songs with me during the playback rehearsals. I heard each song about two times before the takes. But as I said, on all four songs, it was my first take that was used.

That's what tends to happen when you hire pros, especially if the person making the selection picks somebody with the right feel for the job. Plenty of highly competent jazz players could have made the session but failed to find the groove.

Bill continued, "Keith was very friendly and open, as was everyone. You know, this was when they were having the scene with the Hell's Angels."

The aftermath of Altamont was still dragging on, court cases, countersuits, subtle and not-so-subtle threats flying around. A few months later, tour manager Peter Rudge had to fly to New York for "negotiations" with a Hell's Angels spokesman. The Angels were threatening to shoot Jagger onstage during this tour if they didn't get a donation for their clubhouse. And so on. Such was the atmosphere in America in 1972. Bill said, "There was a slight interruption that night with comments they were at the front door. Nothing ever materialized, and there was no trouble of any kind."

It's a pity that the bass in "Turd on the Run" is down so low in the mix—play it with headphones, and check out the range of ideas that fly from the bass.

Jagger's lyric concerns an ingrate who returned affection and gifts of diamonds with an unpleasant social disease. The care he puts into this lyric should be contrasted with that afforded the following track, "Ventilator Blues."

Ventilator Blues Based around a slow bluesy riff—presumably of Mick Taylor's invention, since he gets his sole composing credit on the album— the track smolders but never quite catches fire. Played with a 2/4 feel, you can march to it as easily as dance. A similar tempo to "Sway" from *Sticky Fingers,* though an entirely different beat.

In the key of G, the main riff may have been played on standard or open-tuned guitar, and the tone gives no clue to the player. If we assume that the bottleneck solos were recorded (or played, then later replaced) live, then the main riff is obviously played by Keith. In an interesting variation on Charlie Watt's favorite two-beat drum intro, Jagger leads the track in, placing the rhythmic emphasis of his first words "When yo" exactly where Charlie would have played his two snare beats.

Along with "Rocks Off" this is the only song on *Exile* where everybody plays his own instrument. Just the basic combo—Hopkins, Price, and Keys should be considered honorary members of the eight-piece Stones.

Jagger certainly makes little effort with the lyric. On an album that contains some sensational lyrics, venturing at times into territory that Jagger would normally avoid like the plague, "Ventilator" goes nowhere. The general drift is that everybody needs to let off steam, sometimes, especially when things get tough. One is left with the feeling that this sentiment, or something very similar, has been heard before.

The track segues straight into "I Just Want to See His Face."

I Just Want to See His Face   Another good example of Keith Richards's "vibe" school of writing, "I Just Want to See His Face" is more a feel than a completed song. Owing to its gospel nature—and some fine overdubs in Los Angeles—the band was obviously happy to let it stand as a finished track, where most jams of this type were developed considerably before being considered fit for consumption.

The sense of the shimmering French summer heat at Nellcôte was probably better caught on this track than anywhere else on the album—until Dr. John got his hands on it in L.A., and transformed the song into a piece of sticky, New Orleans backwoods gumbo. Same heat, different location.

Recorded on a steaming hot Sunday on the Riviera, with Keith directing from the Wurlitzer electric piano, Jagger described the scene to Roy Carr: "'I Just Want to See His Face' was another song that I just made up as we went along. Keith was playing the piano one night . . . we set up two mikes, and I made the words up right on the spot."

Later in the same session, or on another day, Mick Taylor added bass guitar and Jimmy Miller provided percussion. Jagger's description may be literal or figurative, but to my ears the bass and percussion sound more like parts of the original session than overdubs.

Either way, the track came to life in L.A., when Bill Plummer added a string bass on top of Mick Taylor's bass guitar, and singers Clydie King, Vanetta Fields, and Jerry Kirkland were brought in to add a gospel feel to the track.

First, they set up a simple, descending three-note accompaniment to the chords and continue it on and off, throughout the track. Second, they join and reinforce Jagger's lead on certain doubled key phrases: in the verses at "Relax your mind" and in the chorus for the title line. The only time they provide a true gospel call and response is at 1:50, where they answer Jagger's "Sometimes you ain't got nobody and you / Want somebody to love."

Gospel is the only word to describe these vocal parts, though whether the final feel is closer to church or to a Creole voodoo incantation is your decision. The track is an undoubted success, and all the better for being left spare.

Let It Loose   A real beauty in every sense, slightly obscured by its location on the album. Whether the final track on disc 3, or track 14 on the CD, so much good music has already gone before it's hard to give this track the full attention it deserves.

An emotional ballad, built around a beautiful guitar figure, the lyric concerns the importance of keeping your emotions concealed (as noted elsewhere, both Jagger and Richards were still Englishmen when this lyric was written). The two key lines are the first, "Who's that woman on your arm, all dressed up to do you harm?" and the last, "Keep those tears hid out of sight, let it loose, let it all come down."

The first verse is sung accompanied only by Mick Taylor's solo guitar (unless it's Keith's solo guitar! It's extremely hard to say for sure). Faint Mellotron string lines from Nicky Hopkins follow Jagger's opening vocal lines, before Hopkins enters on piano. There's a limit to the number of times one can praise Hopkins's piano work—as always, it goes beyond faultless. By mid-track he's playing a sort of cat and mouse game with the guitar part.

I've known this track intimately for twenty-five years, yet never caught half the words until I played it with the lyric sheet in front of me. Phrases

I'd always thought were mere throwaways—"baby," "ooh-yeah," and the like—turn out to be important parts of the narrative. Once you know the lyric, the passion in the vocal makes sense. It's a song about emotion, which derives much of its power from the tension between attempting to control feeling and being overwhelmed by it—"Let it loose, let it all come down."

A fine, impassioned vocal performance by Jagger. Play the track on its own sometime, and concentrate on the vocal. Jagger's tone is good throughout, but in places it's magnificent; listen, for instance, to the force he works into the word "maybe" at 3:40. There's the sound of real passion in the voice.

Not that we should allow ourselves to make any assumptions about the artist's personality from this; the first thing a great soul singer learns to fake is sincerity. We can say, however, that Jagger's sustained perfor-

Mick, Charlie, and Keith at Winterland, San Francisco, in 1972.
(Photo © Larry Hulst/ Michael Ochs Archive, Venice, California)

mance on *Exile* is probably the closest he's ever come to being a true soul singer.

The horns, the Mellotron strings, the large vocal backing group (six people are listed, including Dr. John), and the complicated vocal arrangement all help build the song into a major production, a soul ballad in the Otis tradition. No arranger is credited, but somebody has put a lot of work into the vocal arrangements.

It had become traditional to sink Jagger's voice low in the mix. This device dated back to the days of Andrew Oldham's production, when Jagger's vocals were sometimes a bit iffy—or in his own words, "when I couldn't really sing." A side effect of this was to cast the vocal as "just another of the instruments" rather than the featured element, as with most pop vocals. Speaking to *Melody Maker,* Jagger said, "with the fast ones I really like me voice to be part of the band, but with the slow ones I generally like it upfront a bit." It's well to the fore on this song.

The other Stones tradition—a fine one—has been the absence of a printed lyric sheet, or of lyrics emblazoned on the outer sleeve. There's a formula in pop, a ratio by which the more worthless the lyrics, the more likely they are to be prominently reproduced as part of the packaging. In the Stones' case, you sometimes miss a great line, but this brings the imagination into play. You can fill in the gaps with your own ideas. I like the idea of there being whole passages of a song that you have known and loved for years without having a clue what half the words are.

Jagger told Roy Carr of the *New Musical Express:*

> I never like to print the lyrics. I always think that the lyrics should
> be listened to in the actual context of the song, rather than read as
> a separate piece of poetry. With some songs you might find lyrics
> readable as verse or poetry, but most of the time I think that [ours]
> relate so closely with the music, I just don't feel inclined to sepa-
> rate them.

The musical basis of the song is a beautifully compact guitar figure, creating variations on the sound of the D chord. (In standard tuning, each chord shape has it own unique qualities.) It's really only heard clearly at the start of the song, before the other instruments enter. Richards's (or Taylor's) guitar is fed through a Leslie cabinet (a device intended primarily for the Hammond organ), giving a characteristic "wobble" to its sound. This is a sound Keith was fond of—he used it on, for example, "Comin' Down Again"—but something about the phrasing makes me think that it may be Taylor playing the part.

This figure *seems* to be a three-bar loop, but in fact it's more complex, following the ups and downs of a full verse through twelve bars. The changes are almost subliminal—when they come, they sound entirely natural and only reveal themselves when you try and play along. The song is in F, but its whole tonality comes from the sound of the D chord on a guitar, so we can presume that it's played with a capo at the third fret, raising the D shape to the key of F.

At 5:16, "Let It Loose" is the longest track on the album, but there's an outtake in circulation that features almost six minutes of the backing track alone. Unlike most "karaoke" versions, this is really worth hearing. The main guitar is further forward and its subtleties are easier to hear without the complex vocal arrangement. The first entry of the horn section is something to hear, their tone truly poignant, with a timbre redolent of Memphis. It's well worth looking out for.

Don't mistake it for another outtake, which some identify as a Dallas rehearsal from the 1972 tour, others as a rough version, pre-Nellcôte. This second version is recognizable by the throwaway phrasing of the main guitar riff; most of the grace of the original is lost. After three minutes of kicking the song around, somebody says "Anyone know if we've got a Leslie?" I have no idea where this version was recorded, other than to note that it would seem to be a studio recording (if low-quality), due to the presence of a talkback microphone. Avoid this one, but find the 5:55 "backing track" version.

Once you know the lyric and have heard the backing track from another perspective, you're well placed to appreciate the finished version. Returning to *Exile,* you notice how well the instruments are recorded. Charlie's drums enter sounding particularly crisp, the snare sound as good as it gets. The horns recall Memphis, and the guitar tone is gorgeous.

Play this song on its own sometime, away from the rest of the album—preferably with headphones—and see what's *really* meant by the term "rock ballad."

Side 4

All Down the Line   Another prototypical Stones rocker, "All Down the Line" kicks off side 4 in a similar mood to "Rocks Off" on side 1. One of the songs left over from the *Let It Bleed* sessions at Olympic Studios in July 1969, the song is of roughly the same vintage as "Honky Tonk Women." Recorded again in 1970—same studio, different album—it failed to make its way onto *Sticky Fingers.* Perhaps it never quite settled onto a groove.

The problem here would be matching the excitement of Keith's original demo, played on acoustic guitar. Any full band arrangement would have always been in competition with this early acoustic version, which steams along demonically—a problem similar to the one that bugged the Who whenever they tried to better Pete Townshend's "Magic Bus" demo.

Whether it's a private demo, a first attempt at a master, or one of the takes from Olympic, the acoustic version of "All Down the Line" never fails to galvanize the new listener. The head of steam that's built up by the acoustic guitar, coupled with the poignant quality of the skeleton vocal, is overwhelming.

Featuring Keith on a driving open-tuned acoustic guitar, primitive drum/percussion sounds, and Jagger's sketchy guide vocal, the take is clearly very early. Predating any proper lyric, the vocal mixes the odd complete line (including the title) with a lot of busking: "Oooooooh . . . sha-la la-lay, mah-la-ay." It's a prime example of what Anita called Jagger's ability to interpret the noises Keith makes and turn them into words. Towards the end, a second guitar appears, throwing in some stock "outro" phrases.

Miles away from any sort of completion—little more than an outline—it nonetheless contains everything a track needs to engage the listener. A band is caught in a horrible position when this happens (and most bands get trapped here at least once). Seven or eight musicians and a full vocal fail to match the power of a rough demo. The harder one tries, the worse it gets. Adding extra instrumentation only emphasizes the power of the original. The various different versions in circulation illustrate this point. Nothing beats the original. For raw excitement it has the edge over the finished album version and over several other full-band outtakes.

The *Exile* version adds an intro, a nice piece of picking on the top strings of Keith's open-G guitar. A drum fill from Charlie follows, and in comes the band, the bass pumping eight to the bar and unobtrusively pro-pelling the track forward. Bill Plummer, who's credited with playing dou-ble bass on the track, reckons there are two basses there, an electric *and* his upright bass. Much of the drive comes from the bass(es) that keep the track moving. It's a classic "train" song accompanied by a classic "train" rhythm.

Taylor sits out until the end of the second verse, when he enters with a single, nicely judged slide guitar lick (0:28) phrased very like a blues-harp line. Then he's gone again until 0:48, where a similar phrase brings in the first chorus. Keith's open-tuned chops (rather like "Brown Sugar") are very clear in this first chorus.

Despite a nice tone to the voice and a couple of passages where he really gets moving, Jagger's vocal has a slightly perfunctory air. While well suited to the lyric, this performance never quite recaptures the poignancy of the mumbled, unfinished phrases on the demo. For all the energy expended, the track ends up as a fairly stock Stones rocker; perhaps the reason it never found a place on *Let It Bleed* or *Sticky Fingers.*

The *Exile* version spares nothing in the attempt to make the song kick. Taken at a slightly faster tempo, horns, gospel backing voices, percussion by Jimmy Miller, and Bill Plummer's bass are all thrown in to try and nail the definitive version, but every instrument that's added simply reinforces the dictum "you can't beat simplicity." The demo is just a little slower—completely relaxed—and it sits right in the groove from top to tail.

The song has everything an ideal *Exile* track should (even a coda), but somehow, for me, it just misses the mark. I'm obviously in the minor-ity, however, because the song is a perennial part of the live set. It was even considered as a possible single (it ended up on the B side of the sin-gle "Happy").

Stop Breaking Down   More or less a straight reading of the Robert John-son blues, this number also kicked around at Olympic for some years before fetching up on *Exile*—although in this case there's no magical demo to eclipse the final take. It's listed on at least three different sessions, but that may simply mean it was a favorite warm-up number to jam on.

Roy Carr's review noted, "This is the kind of material on which the Stones really excel." However, you must remember that the *New Musical Express* was getting a real scoop, a preview of the album three weeks

THE ROLLING STONES: EXILE ON MAIN ST.

ahead of the competition, or he might equally well have written, "This is the kind of material which the Stones can knock out in their sleep." Context is everything.

If the Stones at times seemed like a pretty average Camden Town blues band—as they did to Mick Taylor when he first joined in 1969—they've progressed by this point. However, try playing this song side by side with the "Bright Lights, Big City" session—five straight blues recorded at IBC in March 1963—and see which you think sounds fresher.

An uncopyrighted Robert Johnson composition, "Stop Breaking Down" is credited here "Trad. Arr." Jagger/Richards/Wyman/Taylor/Watts, which if not entirely truthful, must surely have eased some of the tensions of band life through the distribution of composing royalties.

The song is mainly a showcase for Mick Taylor, who plays some good bottleneck lead guitar; not Elmore James-style, just "normal" lead guitar lines, played with the slide instead of a finger, to gain extra glissando. In other words, he used a standard tuning rather than the open tuning favored by most slide players. The late Duane Allman preferred this method, and Taylor continues to use it to this day (see Bob Dylan's "Blind Willie McTell" [1983] or any contemporary Mick Taylor show).

For an absolute gem of a solo in this style check the N.Y.C. concert footage of "Love in Vain" from the Maysles brothers' movie *Gimme Shelter*. This is Taylor at his most lyrical. His solo is placed beneath slow-motion footage of Jagger's accompanying balletic twirls, an inspired piece of editing.

A sequence from Robert Frank's unreleased movie of the 1972 U.S. tour, *Cocksucker Blues,* might have benefited from a similar use of slow motion. The footage shows a large Dallas blonde mainlining Keith Richards and then cuts to a dressing-room scene. Slowly and remarkably gracefully, Keith nods out, gradually declining from the perpendicular into the lap of the girl beside him. Perhaps this, rather than the sequence of twelve postcards that accompanied the original LP packaging, is the true scene of The Fall from *Exile on Main St.*

Shine a Light   A remarkable song on several counts, greatly underrated and too often overlooked. Both of the fine songs parked behind "Stop Breaking Down" suffer this problem. How often do you start a CD at track 17? Even when *Exile* was new and vinyl was the only serious format, side 4 of *Exile* seemed the easiest to overlook amid so much good material. Indeed the first record (tracks 1 to 10 on the CD) is so good, it tended to be placed on the turntable far more often than disk 2.

The corollary of opening and closing each (vinyl) side with powerful songs is a tendency for any filler material to get planted in mid-disk (on sides 3 and 4 that's "Ventilator Blues" and "Stop Breaking Down"—worthy, but scarcely earth-shattering tracks).

Unlike *Blonde on Blonde*—the double album traditionally twinned and contrasted with *Exile*—there is no "Sad Eyed Lady" to occupy one complete side, thereby alleviating a quarter of the problem. As a result, "All Down the Line" is often the last track that really sticks in peoples' minds.

It's a good rule to beware of any man, woman, or child who claims that a particular song is "about" them. Even songs that *are* written with an individual in mind often incorporate generalizations, asides, and portions that relate to extraneous relationships. Nevertheless, there's a strong case to be made for "Shine a Light" being a coded love song from Jagger to Keith.

Play the song while you consider this. Annie Leibowitz's photograph of Keith (from the 1972 U.S. tour) slumped out in a chair in full stage drag, eyes closed, with one arm across his chest, makes a perfect visual analogue to this song.

The lyric expresses concern for a close friend who's careless of his acquaintances and lax in his enjoyment of lethal poisons—dangerously lax, in the writer's opinion. The subject is also passionately attached to music. The chorus contains the benediction, "May the Good Lord shine a light on you / Make every song you sing, your favorite tune." Second time around, the last line changes to "Warm like the evening sun," casting long shadows over the remains of the song.

Mick Jagger's lyric is constructed with unusual care. The smile on the face and the tear in the eye of the subject in the first verse match the smiles on the faces and the gleam in the eyes of the angels, whose wingbeats are audible in the last verse as they invite the subject to "come on up" and join them. A lot of work has gone into the details of this lyric, whose predominant themes are love and death.

As far as direct clues go, the subject wears a surfeit of "Berber jew'lry," enough to make them shut their eyes at every *woman* that they meet. Hmmm. Much of Jagger's lasting appeal to both sexes rests on a remarkable ability to combine loutishness with a pronounced feminine sensibility (a winning combination if there ever was one). A girlfriend of mine commented that "the first two verses show a remarkably feminine kind of tenderness—what you feel when you're a girl and you're gazing down on your passed-out loved one—eyes slightly open in that really creepy way—and thinking, 'Isn't he an angel?'"

Now of course this is an old song, the oldest on *Exile;* a contemporary of "Sister Morphine," first recorded in March 1969, when Marianne Faithfull was still in the picture, but that doesn't change a thing. As noted above, a song needn't have a single meaning, or a single inspiration.

Throughout, Jagger refers to the subject as "my sweet honey love." The word "honey" as a term of endearment is usually thought of as twentieth-century American slang. In fact it can be found in Shakespeare, and as far back as Chaucer (400 years before the Declaration of Independence). Both "honey" and "love" were perfectly acceptable terms between straight men in eighteenth- and nineteenth-century English life.

———

"Shine a Light" begins with a quaint little preface—ten seconds of echoed guitar, beneath which close listening will reveal a faint snore, an exhalation, and what's either a grunt or the faintest of attempts at speech (if the latter, then certainly *de profundis*). These, if my thesis is correct, are the sounds of Mr. Keith Richards at rest (though it's always possible they come from the *Satanic Majesties* outtake "Snoring," which featured Bill Wyman).

The song is another prime example of Keith Richards's "something new every ten seconds" method of arranging. Jagger sings the first verse with real soul, accompanied only by piano, which plays a single, sustained block chord on the first beat of each bar. Billy Preston marks off the verse ending with eighth notes low down in the left hand and introduces the second verse ("Berber jew'lry jangling down," etc.) with an overdubbed organ. The two keyboards are joined by an occasional guitar phrase and an irregular high-hat cymbal. This is the first clue that it's Jimmy Miller at the drum kit—Charlie would never have phrased the part this way.

The entry of the whole band is held back until the first chorus: a full minute into the song. At 1:30 the level drops down for the third verse and then picks up a little at 1:53, where the four backing singers sing straight church "ooh's" behind the fourth verse: "Angels beating all their wings in time."

The chorus is followed by an immaculate, melodic guitar solo—Mick Taylor at his free-flying best—which drops into half-time feel for the break-down at 2:58, where Billy Preston uses his fastest possible Leslie setting on the organ to suggest the beating of angelic wings. From here it's a chase until the fade: a chorus, and a second Taylor solo, this one less intense, more reflective.

The session where the basic tracks were laid down was obviously another of those impromptu affairs, with Keith joined by Nellcôte regulars Mick Taylor and Jimmy Miller on bass and drums. The most obvious difference between the drumming of Charlie Watts and Jimmy Miller is the high-hat work and the staggered bass drum pattern. It is far from the regular Stones sound, though it fits the track immaculately. On hearing it, Charlie shrugged his shoulders, decided he couldn't improve on it, and said "leave it."

So many parts were added later in L.A. it's hard to be certain, but the absence of Nicky Hopkins suggests that Keith may have played piano on the basic session. Either way, Billy Preston's L.A. overdubs on both organ and piano create a noticeable change from the Nicky Hopkins piano style that dominates *Exile*.

There are "guitar songs" and "piano songs," and everything indicates that "Shine a Light" was written at the piano. Two easily found outtakes illuminate this. The first is identifiable by its count-in, "A-one two three," and collapses at 4:20 with Jagger remarking, "That was quite noice." Mick Taylor's bottleneck part is prominent, and there's no rhythm guitar. The song is definitely led from the piano, though whether it's Keith leading is difficult to tell (he could be playing bass). The piano could be Ian Stewart—or even Nicky Hopkins caught in an unguarded moment—but something faintly clumsy about the playing makes me think it's Keith, perhaps teaching the song to Taylor. This would suggest it's the 1969 Olympic take. Jagger's lyrics are close to the *Exile* version (only the word "shine" tends to be replaced by "flash"); his vocal phrasing is less so.

The second version is far closer to the finished product, an outtake from the L.A. sessions. Most of the master elements are in place. The final piano and organ are down, the lead vocal is a different take, though the performance is close to the finished version. The major difference is the lead guitar.

Mick Taylor gets off two exquisite solos, the first at 2:31, the second at 3:36. Both are spur-of-the-moment improvised solos, although several key phrases and the overall shaping—the rises and falls—resemble the finished version. It's clear that he has his part pretty much worked out and is just running off solos until one special take stands out. Taylor's tone is more bluesy—a dab more reverb is added and he's higher in the mix, which makes more difference than you'd suppose. This outtake offers as definitive a piece of Stones-period Mick Taylor as you'll find anywhere, and is a must for Taylor fans.

Billy Preston, contributor of many a tasty lick, onstage with Jagger, 1975. (PHOTO: CORBIS/ NEAL PRESTON)

Soul Survivor An amusing set of lyrics are lost here, for two reasons. Last in a line of eighteen songs is not an advantageous position for any song (consider how this would have stood out as the third track on side 1). Second, though the lyric is not buried that far down in the mix, Jagger reverts to his "mouthful-of-marbles" diction, in the style of "Stray Cat Blues." This is a wonderful rock 'n' roll noise and offers great entertainment value, but it does not always help convey meaning.

The lyric extends nautical imagery (though you would be forgiven for not having noticed) about as far as a three-and-a-half-minute pop tune will support. A phrase in the opening verse that I would always heard as "front-row view" is actually "cut-throat crew." During the course of twenty-five years' enjoyable listening, in fact, I find I've been happily misreading five

of the seven lines that make up the first verse—without the slightest diminution of enjoyment. It doesn't matter a bit.

When you do eventually listen with a lyric sheet (and there are many available over the Internet), the verses are something of a revelation. Jagger makes a particularly good job of fitting the phonetics to the melody—listen to the line "I'd rather drink sea-water." In speech the stress would fall on the word sea; as rendered here by Jagger, we get "drinksy oughta," a fine example of the folly of trying to separate the sung and the written word.

The song's emotional punch comes in the line "Where you are, I won't be," which precedes the refrain "Gonna be the death of me." If you wonder precisely what quality reviewer Richard Williams had in mind when he wrote of Jagger's "authority," you'll find it (among other places) in this song.

For all its piratical swagger, the lyric concerns getting away. The lover in this song is simply too much. He/she is someone to be avoided, even at the cost of running away to sea. The stud who would once have crushed her under his thumb now frankly admits that "his confidence sags"—which is why he's packing his bags.

Musically the track is a clear "guitar song," written in straightforward open-G tuning, with an uncomplicated structure. The main elements are heard most clearly in the first verse; Keith's founding chords are doubled by Mick Taylor's bottleneck guitar, with Nicky Hopkins's barrelhouse piano providing texture. Charlie holds the track down so smoothly you hardly notice, and by now, anyone who's been paying attention will hear that it's not Bill Wyman on bass. Gotta be Mick Taylor or Keith. As it turns out, it's Keith, though either could have done the job.

At 2:13 the track halts, and Nicky Hopkins sets a nice little piano vibe going. More authority, and all the better for its apparent effortlessness. Played solo (apart from some simple percussion), its two-handed syncopation follows no rhythm that has yet occurred in the track. Nonetheless, when Keith's main open-tuned riff reenters over the top, it's a perfect fit.

Slow fade, baritone sax stabs, Micks Jagger and Taylor weaving lines around the girls' repeated chorus cry "Soul Survivor." Underneath it all, the Stones' true rhythm section, Keith and Charlie, hold everything in place.

As ever.

Harpsucker blues.
(Photo: Corbis/
Neal Preston)

THE REVIEWS

Whenever leading rock magazines poll their readers for the "hundred greatest albums of all time," there are a handful of albums you can count on, without fail, to turn up in the Top 20. Such polls don't always recognize the subtler nuances of rock 'n' roll—a media event like *Sgt. Pepper* almost always trumps the album that many fans, most critics (and for that matter, most Beatles themselves) recognize as their best, namely *Revolver.* But any respectable poll can usually be counted on to include the Stones' double albums *Blonde on Blonde* and *Exile on Main St.*

Psephologists would point out the distortion caused by current favorites at the time of polling. Thus a 1997 poll in *Q* magazine pronounced the greatest album of all time to be *OK Computer* by Radiohead—one of that year's better albums, to be sure, but likely to be something of an outsider for the number-1 spot in any year other than that of its release.

Among the hard core of regulars that appear decade after decade—*Pet Sounds, Blonde on Blonde, Sgt. Pepper*—it's hard to think of any album whose release prompted, and continues to prompt, quite such a mixed critical reception as *Exile on Main St.* Of course, many other great albums have been greeted by less-than-laudatory reviews. The mighty *Blood on the Tracks,* an album that several ranking Dylanologists rate as his finest, was panned by *Melody Maker* (who also greeted *Sgt. Pepper* in fairly negative terms).

When *Exile on Main St.* was released, even diehard Stones' supporters penned reviews that mixed puzzlement with *qualified* praise, a view that sometimes appears undiminished by the passage of time. There are two good examples. First, there is Robert Christgau's considered critique written in 1982 for his book *Rock Albums of the '70s,* in which he comments that "this fagged-out masterpiece is difficult—how else to describe music that takes weeks to understand? Weary and complicated, barely afloat in its own drudgery, it rocks with extra power and concentration as a result. A plus." Second, Victor Bockris, writing with the benefit of long hindsight, said that "many elements combined to make *Exile* a raw, flawed, masterpiece."

Christgau is spot on with A plus, but what takes weeks to understand? To each his own, but I can truthfully say that *Exile on Main St.* grabbed me as immediately as any record I've ever heard. Just as many people can remember exactly where they were at moments of collective national calamity—like the day that Billie Joe McAllister jumped off the Tallahachee Bridge—I can recall every detail of my first meet with *Exile.* OK, so it was my birthday. It was a beautiful sunny day in early June and I was just leaving my teens. A friend brought the album over and put it on the turntable. The needle hit the opening chords of "Rocks Off," and the blood pumped straight to my head.

The disk ended and somebody turned it over. A whole new feel. A pastoral side. Here was a record I *knew* I was gonna be playing in twenty years' time—a mixture of music that not only hit straight off ("Jumpin' Jack Flash" had done that), but also defined exactly what I wanted to play *myself.* "Sweet Virginia" led into "Torn and Frayed." Enough, I was sold. In many respects still an innocent at age 20, I *had* been a professional musician for five years, and here on "Torn and Frayed," over simple chords played the way I played, were lyrics that made *personal* sense to me. Not just filler, clever rhyme, or Jagger's mannered posturing, but lyrics that were true to life—to my life, anyway.

Sticky Fingers had been enjoyable, but it never spoke to me like this. I'd never sailed slave ships or whipped the women, just before midnight or at any other time of the day (a chap should save *something* for his twenty-first). I'd never placed bets on Kentucky Derby Day or received dead flowers through the mail. I was scarcely on nodding terms with Sister Morphine or her relatives. My experience of the scene that *Sticky Fingers* celebrated was so slight as to be scarcely worth acknowledging—but I was very familiar with that same circuit of ballrooms (if less so with the bordellos) and dressing rooms filled with parasites, both insect and human.

Sticky Fingers was hewn from much the same rock as *Exile on Main St.* (chronologically, the sessions overlap and intermingle like nobody's business) but somehow it sounded *assembled; Exile* sounded as though it had always been there. *Sticky Fingers* contained great music—a marvelous single in "Brown Sugar," a hint of side-2 *Exile* country-and-western in "Dead Flowers," country blues in Mississippi Fred McDowells's "You Gotta Move," an exquisite ballad in "Wild Horses," an open-tuned masterpiece of a riff in "Can't You Hear Me Knocking"—but all so *neat,* so clean. Experiencing it was like being onboard a luxury liner, sheltered from the thunder of the engines, whereas *Exile on Main St.* sounded like it was recorded in the boiler room.

Jimmy Miller summed up the production values: "Conceptually the album is away from the studio. The idea was to try and get back to good old rock 'n' roll." And Jagger—back in those days when he could sometimes still be counted on to make a plain statement without immediately qualifying it—summed the whole thing up perfectly. "*Sticky Fingers* was a bit 'London,'" he said. "It should've been called *Too Long in London.*"

From a single listening, *Exile on Main St.* sounded like a masterpiece, or as close to that imprecise term as makes no difference. At gut level, it rocked as hard as any Stones album, but it left the impression that if you chose to look deeper into it, there was more to find. Was I alone with such an immediate response? I somehow doubt it.

When you compare reviews, the single greatest difference between the English and American perspectives has to do with interpretation of the Stones' role. Are they a pop group or prophets? Are they song and dance men or shamans? American reviewers tended to take the lyrics and the postures much more seriously, more literally, investing the band's symbolism and imagery with a far greater weight of significance than was customary in Britain.

Don Heckman's largely favorable review for the *New York Times* includes a psychoanalytical critique—the Stones as collective *id* for an entire generation, a thoughtful, moderated, intellectual, East Coast version of the "practicing Satanists" view that had flourished in the West, especially around San Francisco, after the December 1969 debacle at Altamont.

The *moderate* voices in *Rolling Stone* magazine's "Altamont Special Issue" (January 1970) spoke of "diabolical egotism, hype, ineptitude, money manipulation and at base, a fundamental lack of concern for

humanity." No lesser fount of humility, humanitarianism, and altruism than the saintly David Crosby pronounced that the "Stones are still a little bit in 1965. They didn't really know that security isn't a part of anybody's concert anywhere anymore. [They] are on star trips and qualify in my book as snobs. I think they are on negative trips intensely, especially the two leaders." Good ol' Dave, always the first to play to the gallery.

There's no doubting the impact of Altamont on American perceptions of the Stones. It's just a pity that the loudest voices shouting about "Sympathy for the Devil" were those who had the least idea what the song was about. For everyone who had read *The Master and Margarita,* there were ten ready to believe diabolical pacts and devil worship.

The San Francisco band who showed the greatest presence of mind at Altamont were the Grateful Dead. The Maysles brothers' footage shows Garcia and Lesh making the wisest move of the day, turning straight around and going home the minute they learned what was happening—yet despite the denials, they were deeply implicated in the presence of the Hell's Angels. Sam Cutler from the Stones and Rock Scully from the Dead are usually held as the traditional villains of the piece. When I spoke to Scully in 1981 he denied responsibility vehemently—but then he would, wouldn't he? I liked Scully, but I cannot honestly say that, plausible though they sounded at the time, even one of the reasons he outlined for his lack of culpability have remained with me.

It's a salutary reminder of the mood of those times that people like Jann Wenner were prepared to give credence to opinions such as those below, by publishing them in *Rolling Stone:*

> To those who know, Jagger has been involved in the practice of Magick since *Their Satanic Majesties.* At Altamont, He appeared in his full Majesty with his full consort of demons, the Hell's Angels. It was just a few days before the winter solstice, when the powers of darkness are at their most powerful. The moon was in Scorpio—the time of the month when the universal vibration is at its most unstable. Then Mick comes on only after it is dark enough for the red lights to work their magick.

And so on. Hubris, nemesis—reds, acid, speed . . .

Contrary to the wisdom of California's leading astrologers, the Stones were not waiting for the Satanic powers to wax at Altamont, for the propitious moment when the moon formed an exact and suitably malefic aspect to Saturn and Mars—but rather, for their bassist, Mr. Bill Wyman, who was still at his hotel in San Francisco. Altamont, and the storm of press that followed it, took place as 1969 gave way to 1970, and the release of *Exile on Main St.* coincided with the Stones' first American tour since the fatal night. As anticipation mounted, it seemed that remarkably little had changed in the outlook of the American underground press.

Two years on, broadly the same view of the function of rock music as a whole appears in Lenny Kaye's *Rolling Stone* review of *Exile,* which alludes to a "spectral community alchemy" through which we, the audience, have "chosen the Stones to bring our darkness into light." Lenny concludes that the Stones are treading water and that perhaps their next record will be better.

Music affects us so immediately precisely *because* it engages us directly, bypassing language. If it works for you, it works. That's the only "truth." The rest is interpretation, opinion, and journalists looking to carve themselves a rep. Only when we try to convey this in speech or in writing do we find people tying themselves up in knots. When a band repeatedly succeeds in engaging us so completely; when a concert moves a mass of people into some sort of communal space, there are a number of symbolic ways of describing the sensation, and the vocabulary of "magic" *is* one of the options available to us—but it's a terrible mistake to confuse the symbols with life. If it makes your life more bearable to believe that Robert Johnson really did cut a bargain with the devil to save money on guitar lessons, that's your choice.

So much for the issue of Magick. One man's warlock is another man's old tart in a Mr. Fish frock.

While the American press was getting worked up about occultism and the demise of the 1960s ethos, the British papers felt that the reliable combination of sex and drugs sold more papers. As wide of the mark as their American counterparts, they tended to play the Beatles off against the Stones.

A major part of the Stones' "dark side" mythology derived from their very public flaunting of class-A narcotics, principally cocaine and heroin, which began to feature prominently on *Sticky Fingers* (1971)—heads full of snow, sister morphine, and so on—although this only reflected the tastes of the Stones' two principal songwriters. Yet well-placed insiders at Abbey Road Studios suggest that all four Beatles were snorting speedballs (a mixture of heroin and cocaine) throughout the making of *Sgt. Pepper* (1967), a period when (despite the Redlands pot bust) the Stones were still openly deriding Brian Jones as a washed up "druggie."

Similarly, public perception throughout the 1960s of what Shirley Watts called the "three big bad stones"—Brian, Keith, and Mick—was way off the mark. Depicted in the British press as satyrs, even within their own group the "big three" were eclipsed by Bill Wyman (who kept a scorecard). Scandalous activity on Stones tours certainly never exceeded that of the parallel Beatles tours, which insiders likened to "Roman orgies." But this sort of bogus duality suited journalistic requirements and satisfied a public sense of neatness, so the "nice" Beatles were balanced by the "nasty" Stones.

So many different ways to miss the point—at base, all caused by thinking too much instead of just *listening*. The case for the defense is best put by Jagger himself, previewing the album to Roy Carr at *New Musical*

Express, after the final mixes but before the release of (and reaction to) *Exile on Main St.:* "I hope the people . . . aren't gonna sit back. I hope they're gonna dance. It's such a danceable record, don't you think? It's not really a thinking man's record."

Rolling Stones: "Exile on Main Street" (Rolling Stones Records)
BY RICHARD WILLIAMS
Melody Maker (London), May 27, 1972

The really memorable albums come out during two seasons of the year: a couple of weeks before Christmas, or at the beginning of the summer.

The first lot see you through the parties and youth-club hops ("With the Beatles"), while the second come blasting out of open windows, reflecting off the baked concrete and over the beach ("Pet Sounds"). "Exile on Main Street" is definitely going to be one of the latter, one that's going to hang around all summer before moving off to take its place in history.

It is, I think, the best album they've made—which is particularly remarkable because it's a double album, and consistency has never been the Stones' forte. Their old albums were rounded out by nondescript fillers, while the goodies were always spinning at 45rpm. But, unbelievably as they approach their 30s they're just getting better and better, losing none of the arrogance and adding a musical maturity which doesn't prejudice the inherent raunch. This is all the more suprising when you consider their near-Establishment status. How come Mick's society wedding doesn't take the edge off his style? No one knows. Just be glad it doesn't.

Oddly, despite its length, "Exile" doesn't have the musical scope of "Sticky Fingers"; instead they've focused the music far more tightly, coming up with an album which rocks all the way down. Dotted throughout are a number of great stompers: "Rocks Off," "Rip This Joint," "Tumbling Dice," "Soul Survivor," "Casino Boogie," "Turd on the Run," "Happy," and the apocalyptic "All Down the Line," a natural-born chart-topper if I ever heard one. All these tracks are witness to the immensely gifted and curiously under-rated Keith Richards whose rhythm guitar work is the spark which ignites the fire. Richards has adapted and coarsened the Chuck Berry approach, and is capable of swinging the band on his own—which is the function of a rhythm guitarist, from Freddie Green through Steve Cropper.

Mick Taylor is a fine complement, adding neat little slide fills and the occasional brief solo, while Wyman and Watts are surely unique in the complete absence of licks in their playing—it's just straight-ahead swing. Bobby Keys, Jim Price, and Nicky Hopkins flesh out the sound, and there's a fair selection of backing singers: Clydie, Vanetta, Kathi, Tammi, etc. The enigmatically-named Amyl Nitrate turns up to play marimbas on "Sweet Black Angel," one of the quieter songs, dedicated to Angela Davis. Among the other pace-changers are the strangely unresolved "Just Wanna See His Face," the autobiographical "Torn and Frayed," and the long, dense "Let It Loose."

Throughout, Jagger's voice maintains the kind of taut authority which he hasn't always commanded, slipping into unnecessary affectation only on Slim Harpo's "Hip Shake." That aside, this is an album which utterly repulses the sneers and arrows of outraged put-down artists. Once and for all, it answers any questions about their ability as rock 'n' rollers.

"Tumbling Dice" Puts the Cherry on the First Side of "Main Street"
By Lenny Kaye
Rolling Stone (San Francisco), July 6, 1972

There are songs that are better, there are songs that are worse, there are songs that'll become your favorites and others you'll probably lift the needle for when their time is due. But in the end, *Exile on Main Street* (Rolling Stones COC-2-2900) spends its four sides shading the same song in as many variations as there are Rolling Stones readymades to fill them, and if on the one hand they prove the group's eternal constancy and appeal, it's on the other that you can leave the album and still feel vaguely unsatisfied, not quite brought to the peaks that this band of bands has always held out as a special prize in the past.

The Stones have never set themselves in the forefront of any musical revolution, instead preferring to take what's already been laid down and then gear it to its highest most slashing level. Along this road they've displayed a succession of sneeringly-believable poses, in a tradition so grand that in lesser hands they could have become predictable, coupled with an acute sense of social perception and the kind of dynamism that often made everything else seem beside the point.

Through a spectral community alchemy, we've chosen the Stones to bring our darkness into light, in each case via a construct that fits the time and prevailing mood perfectly. And, as a result, they alone have become the last of the great hopes. If you can't bleed on the Stones, who *can* you bleed on?

Final night of the 1972 US tour, New York City.
(PHOTO: JOE SIA, STAR FILE)

In that light, *Exile on Main Street* is not just another album, a two-month binge for the rack jobbers and then onto whoever's up next. Backed by an impending tour and a monumental picture book, its mere presence in record stores makes a statement. And as a result, the group has been given a responsibility to their audience which can't be dropped by the wayside, nor should be, given the two-way street on which music always has to function. Performers should not let their public make career decisions for them, but the best artisans of any era have worked closely within their audience's expectations, either totally transcending them (the Beatles in their up-to-and including *Sgt. Pepper* period) or manipulating them (Dylan, continually).

The Stones have prospered by making the classic assertion whenever it was demanded of them. Coming out of *Satanic Majesties Request,* the unholy trio of "Jumpin' Jack Flash," "Street Fighting Man," and "Sympathy for the Devil" were the blockbusters that brought them back in the running. After, through "Midnight Rambler," "Honky Tonk Women," "Brown Sugar," "Bitch," and those jagged edge opening bars of "Can't You Hear Me Knocking," they've never failed to make that affirmation of their superiority when it was most needed, of the fact that others may come and go but the Rolling Stones will always be.

This continual topping of one's self can only go on for so long, after which one must sit back and sustain what has already been built. And with *Exile on Main Street,* the Stones have chosen to sustain for the moment, stabilizing their pasts and presenting few directions for their future. The fact that they do it so well is testament to one of the finest bands in the world. The fact that they take a minimum of chances, even given the room of their first double album set, tends to dull that finish a bit.

Exile on Main Street is the Rolling Stones at their most dense and impenetrable. In the tradition of Phil Spector, they've constructed a wash of sound in which to frame their songs, yet where Spector always aimed to create an impression of space and airiness, the Stones group everything together in one solid mass, providing a tangled jungle through which you have to move toward the meat of the material. Only occasionally does an instrument or voice break through to the surface, and even then it seems subordinate to the ongoing mix, and without the impact that a break in the sound should logically have.

One consequence of this style is that most of the hard-core action on the record revolves around Charlie Watts' snare drum. The sound gives him room not only to set the pace rhythmically but to also provide the bulk of the drive and magnetism. Another is that because Jagger's voice has been dropped to the level of just another instrument, burying him even more than usual, he has been freed from any restrictions the lyrics might have once imposed. The ulterior motives of mumbling aside, with much of the record completely unintelligible—though the words I could make out generally whetted my appetite to hear more—he's been left with something akin to pure singing, utilizing only his uncanny sense of style to carry him home from there. His performances here are among the finest he's graced us with in a long time, a virtual drama which amply proves to me that there's no other vocalist who can touch him, note for garbled note.

As for Keith, Bill and Mick T. their presence comes off as subdued, never overly apparent until you put your head between the speakers. In the case of the last two, this is perfectly understandable. Wyman has never been a front man, and his bass has never recorded with an eye to clarity. He's the bottom, and he fulfils his support role with a grace that is unfailingly admirable. Mick Taylor falls about the same, chosen to take Brian's place as much because he could be counted on to stay in the background as for his perfect counterpoint guitar skills. With Keith, however, except for a couple of spectacular chording exhibitions and some lethal openings, his instrument wizardry is practically nowhere to be seen, unless you happen to look particularly hard behind Nicky Hopkins' piano or the dual horns of Price/Keys. It hurts the album, and the bone earring has often provided the marker on which the Stones rise or fall.

Happily, though, *Exile on Main Street* has the Rolling Stones sounding like a full-fledged five-into-one band. Much of the self-consciousness that marred *Sticky Fingers* has apparently vanished, as well as that album's tendency to touch every marker on the Hot 100. It's been replaced by a tight focus on basic components of the Stones' sound as we've always known it, knock-down rock and roll stemming from blues, backed with a pervading feeling of blackness that the Stones have seldom failed to handle well.

The album begins with "Rocks Off," a prototypical Stones opener whose impact is greatest in its first 15 seconds. Kicked off by one of Richards' patented guitar scratchings, a Jagger aside and Charlie's sharp crack, it moves into the kind of song the Stones have built a reputation on, great choruses and well-judged horn bursts, painlessly running you through the motions until you're out of the track and into the album. But if that's one of its assets, it also stands for one of its deficiencies—there's nothing distinctive about the tune. Stones' openers of the past have generally served to set the mood for the mayhem to follow: this one tells you that we're in for nothing new.

"Rip This Joint" is a stunner, getting down to the business at hand with the kind of music the Rolling Stones were born to play. It starts at a pace that yanks you into its locomotion full tilt, and never lets up from there, the sax solo is the purest of rock and roll. Slim Harpo's "Shake Your Hips" mounts up another plus, with a fine mannered vocal from Jagger. The guitars are the focal point here, and they work with each other like a pair of Corsican twins. "Casino Boogie" sounds at times as if it were a Seventies remake from the chord progression of "Spider and the Fly" and for what it's worth, I suppose I'd rather listen to "jump right ahead in my web" any day.

But it's left to "Tumbling Dice" to not just place a cherry on the first side, but to also provide one of the album's only real moves towards a classic. As the guitar figure slowly falls into Charlie's inevitable smack, the song builds to the kind of majesty the Stones at their best have always provided. Nothing is out of place here, Keith's simple guitar figure providing the nicest of bridges, the chorus touching the upper levels of heaven and spurring on Jagger, set up by an arrangement that is both unique and imaginative. It's definitely the cut that deserved the single, and the fact that it's not likely to touch number one shows we've perhaps come a little further than we originally intended.

Side two is the only side on *Exile* without a barrelhouse rocker, and drags as a result. I wish for once the Stones could do a country song in the way they've apparently always wanted, without feeling the need to hoke it up in some fashion. "Sweet Virginia" is a perfectly friendly lazy shuffle that gets hung on an overemphasized "shit" in the chorus. "Torn and Frayed" has trouble getting started, but as it inexorably rolls to its code the Stones find their flow and relax black, allowing the tune to lovingly expand. "Sweet Black Angel," with its vaguely West Indian rhythm and Jagger playing Desmond Dekker comes off as a pleasant experiment that works, while "Loving Cup" is curiously faceless, though it must be admitted the group works enough out-of-the-ordinary breaks and bridges to give it at least a fighting chance; the semi-soul fade on the end is rhythmically satisfying but basically undeveloped, adding in the cut's lack of impression.

The third side is perhaps the best organized of any on *Exile.* Beginning with the closest thing to a pop number Mick and Keith have written on the album, "Happy" lives up to its title from start to finish. It's a natural-born single, and its position as a side opener seems to suggest the group thinks so too. "Turd on the Run," even belying its gimmicky title, is a superb little hustler; if Keith can be said to have a showpiece on the album, this is it. Taking off from a jangle "Maybellene" rhythm guitar, he misses not a flick of the wrist, sitting behind the force of the instrumental and shovelling it along. "Ventilator Blues" is all Mick, spreading the guts of his voice all over the microphone, providing an entrance into the gumbo ya-ya of "I Just Want to See His Face," Jagger and the chorus sinuously wavering around a grand collection of jungle drums. "Let It Loose" closes out the side, and as befits the album's second claim to classic, is one beautiful song, both lyrically and melodically. Like on "Tumbling Dice," everything seems to work as a body here, the gospel chorus providing tension, the leslie'd guitar rounding the mysterious nature of the track, a great performance from Mick and just the right touch of backing instruments. Whoever that voice belongs to hanging off the fade in the end, I'd like to kiss her right now: she's that lovely.

Coming off "Let It Loose," you might expect side four to be the one to really put the album on the target. Not so. With the exception of an energy-ridden "All Down the Line" and about half of "Shine a Light," *Exile* starts a slide downward which happens so rapidly you might be left a little dazed as to what exactly happened. "Stop Breaking Down" is such an overdone blues cliché that I'm surprised it wasn't placed on *Jamming With Edward.* "Shine a Light" starts with perhaps the best potential of any song on the album, a slow, moody piece with Mick singing in a way calculated to send chills up your spine. Then, out of nowhere, the band segues into the kind of shlock gospel song that Tommy James has already done better. Then they move you back into the slow piece. Then back into shlock gospel again. It's enough to drive you crazy.

After four sides you begin to want some conclusion to the matters at hand, to let you off the hook so you can start all over fresh. "Soul Survivor," though a pretty decent and upright song in itself, can't provide the kind of kicker that is needed at this point. Its typicality, within the *oeuvre* of the Rolling Stones, means it could've been placed anywhere, and with "Let It Loose" just begging to seal the bottle, there's no reason why it should be the last thing left you by the album.

Still, talking about the pieces of *Exile on Main Street* is somewhat off the mark here, since individually the cuts seem to stand quite well. Only when they're taken together, as a lump sum of four sides, is their impact blunted. This would be all right if we were talking about any other group but the Stones. Yet when you've been given the best, it becomes hard to accept anything less, and if there are few moments that can be faulted on this album, it also must be said that the magic high spots don't come as rapidly.

Exile on Main Street appears to take up where *Sticky Fingers* left off, with the Stones attempting to deal with their problems and once again slightly missing the mark. They've progressed to the other side of the extreme, wiping out one set of solutions only to be confronted with another. With few exceptions, this has meant that they've stuck close to home, doing the sort of things that come naturally, not stepping out of the realm in which they feel most comfortable. Undeniably it makes for some fine music, and it surely is a good sign to see them recording so prolifically again; but I still think that the great Stones album of their mature period is yet to come. Hopefully, *Exile on Main Street* will give them the solid footing they need to open up, and with a little horizon-expanding (perhaps honed by two months on the road), they might even deliver it to us the next time around.

Hot Summer on Main St.
By Norm Jopling
Record Mirror (London), June 4, 1972

Whatever it is they've got, the Rolling Stones haven't lost it. "Exile on Main Street" is a great record packed with energy, excitement and repetition. Someone once said—and I think it was me—that there wasn't a two-lp set around that wouldn't have been better as a single album. "Blonde on Blonde" was the quick reply, and although some of the makeweights should have been bootlegged, the set will probably improve the world climate in summer 1972. Down, Don McLean!

First time I heard it, it was in mono. At least, I was in the kitchen getting some grub together so all that mixing that bugged Mick was wasted.

And anyway, it was at a friend's place whose stereo is one of those expensive trendy all-white systems with the controls in Deutsche. It makes everything sound like it was being played on a stereo telephone, if such an object exists.

Immediate impressions—much better production than ever before, especially after the patchy "Sticky Fingers." Lost of styles and influences, but unlike the Beatles' pristine white double album, it works much more on the physical level—it ain't so much of an immaculate head trip.

Everything is heard and seen through the wall of decadent booshwah-R&B that they erected a long time ago . . . certain tracks were probably conceived as items of fair musical purity in their individual styles, but as the songs go through the interminable process they all end up coated with the same wash. With many of the songs there's a real aleph quality—the influences stretch back and back, not to the real roots but to the Stones' own landmarks, with "Come On," "Not Fade Away," "Satisfaction," "Jumpin' Jack Flash," and "Honky Tonk Women" contained somewhere in most of them. It's incestuous, but you know what you're getting.

Many of the tracks are absolutely tremendous. They work on the traditional blues "Stop Breaking Down," and while Mick invests the vocals with a leering interpretation of Robert Johnson (which is pretty nice and straight), the rest of the gang pound away with a baroque series of savage blues rhythms overlaid with a lovely guitar.

"Black Angel" is a calypso-based bit of whimsy, the dark side of "Brown Sugar," and they make it sound suitably diabolical—especially with the well-known shaker Amyl Nitrate on marimbas. Other really good tracks are the opener "Rocks Off" and the easy rolling "Sweet Virginia," an especially good song with an atmosphere like a dirty "Barbara Ann."

Cover art—as usual—is "shocking" and inventive, but doesn't quite make it, unlike the series of picture-postcards inside which are a gas, providing you read one every two days and don't waste them on your friends. A few forecasts will come down if this set sells well—not only is there a gatefold cover, but each album has its own individual sleeve and inner sleeve too.

The Stones have gone on and on churning out the same music, and they've reached a definite peak here. I suppose they could go on even further, getting the production that much cleaner, the cover that much more like real Pop art, the sax that much more King Curtis, the songs that much more cutting and refined. But Mick has been moaning about groups making the same old sounds and claims he still digs "Satanic Majesties" and wants to go in new directions. Fair enough—I'd love another experiment like "Satanic Majesties." Yet this LP is what they're good at, and what no-one else can beat them at. A dilemma, perhaps. And Exile on Main Street for sure.

Mick and Keith Soften the Stones
BY DON HECKMAN
New York Times, June 4, 1972

The Rolling Stones are on the West Coast this weekend, about to embark on their first concert tour since the disastrous events at Altamont. The timing obviously was right for the release of a new album, and the Stones have obliged with a far-ranging two-disk collection called *Exile on Main Street* (Rolling Stones Records COC-2-2900).

The recordings are perhaps the best cross-section yet of the unique elements that make up the Stones' music. Actually, it is not so much the elements themselves that are unique as the way they go together. Three primal sources are tapped by Mick Jagger and Keith Richards when they devise their material: black blues, usually of the style associated with the Mississippi Delta area in the mid-thirties; Southern gospel music; and, less well-defined, early sixties English rock 'n' roll.

Other groups, of course, have based their styles on a similar synthesis, and one might make a case for black blues and gospel as the foundation—the very substance—of virtually *all* rock 'n' roll music. But the Stones clearly have put the pieces together in a way that comes out sounding unique. The style may be familiar but the substance is unidentifiable as anything except the Rolling Stones.

Jagger's voice contributes a large part of the uniqueness—a hoarse, whining sound that blurs the words and sneers with arrogant self-righteousness. Richards' firm musical control is less obvious but, I suspect, equally important. The current attitude of the Rolling Stones—it was not always true in the past—is to stick to basics; rhythms are simple and repetitious, melodies are little more than chanted riffs, and the textures add only a few dashes of coloration to the guitar-based rock sound. The Stones' past obsession with lyrics has lapsed to the extent that Jagger's voice is usually placed well back into the instrumental sound, making many of the lyrics unintelligible; perhaps intentionally, no lyric sheet has been included with the album, so the listener is on his own if he decides to search for significance in the words.

The pieces range over the Stones' spectrum of styles: straight-ahead hard rock in "Happy," "All Down the Line," "Soul Survivor," "Rocks Off" and "Loving Cup"; a trace of gospel (assisted in no small measure by the presence of Billy Preston on organ and piano) in "Shine a Light"; all sorts of boogie, from jumping forties' jazz style to more contemporary rock-blues-boogie, in numbers like "Rip This Joint," "Hip Shake," "Casino Boogie," "Tumbling Dice" and "Turd on the Run"; slow, blues-based tunes that showcase Jagger like "Ventilator Blues," "Let It Loose" and "Stop Breaking Down"; more unusual items like the reggae styled "Black Angel," a folky, Dylan-styled "Sweet Virginia" and a surprisingly soul-sounding "Just Wanna See His Face."

Where, you might ask, are the Stones of old, the street-fightin' sympathizers with the devil? One wonders. The album's cover—a collection of candid photos of human "freaks," midgets, fat women, cripples, etc. are on the front jacket, candid photos of the Stones are on the back—may provide a clue. The largely frustrated energies directed at social change (or, less grandiosely, toward a public expression of outrage) in past Stones' albums seem to have diffused into smaller, more personal gestures of finger pointing. It's as though Jagger and Richards had decided that uncovering the spreading rot beneath a single rock might be a bit more effective than trying to change the world. And so Jagger screams small obscenities and outlines little violences. No, it isn't what the Stones of 1969 might have done, but who is to say that it will be any less effective than, say, "Street Fightin' Man"?

The Rolling Stones have played the role of a kind of universal id for a generation of young people; thoughts, feelings and attitudes that had never before been quite speakable were expressed—outspokenly, even arrogantly—in the Stones' music, and the effect was incredibly cathartic. But the Stones, and their fans, discovered that the unleashed, unfocused energy of the id can stimulate darker deeds as well. The softened intensity in what the Stones do and say in this new album reflects, I think, that those who play the role of public symbols—totems, if you will—bear responsibilities.

It certainly hasn't reduced the Stones' musical effectiveness. Social significances aside, this has always been one of the premiere rock 'n' roll groups—the kind of band that would get people out of their seats and into the aisles even if they were called the Sussex Stompers. "Exile on Main Street" has enough rock music, of all shades and styles, to make anyone happy. And if you insist upon revolutionary manifestos, try listening closely to some of the lyrics. The Stones are looking inward now, and if they help you to understand something about yourself, that just might be the most revolutionary act of all.

A Track by Track of the Upcoming "Exile on Main Street"
Set Three Weeks before Release
BY ROY CARR
New Musical Express (London), April 29, 1972

Side One

Rocks Off (Jagger/Richard) 4:33 mins.   A tremendous opener, spotlighting Jagger's forceful voice as it punches against a solid wall of guitar and Nicky Hopkins's raw jangled piano.

Extremely reminiscent of Dylan with the Band circa 1966 (the brass pick up the riff after a couple of choruses and the production evolves into one great big ball of sound) this neo-erotic song hooks around the chorus: "I only get my rocks off while I'm dreaming / I only get my rocks off while I'm sleeping"; chugs on until it reaches a phased interlude and then harks back to the feel of the "Satanic Majesties" collection before rockin' off once again.

Rip This Joint (Jagger/Richard) 2:24 mins.   A wild eight-to-the-bar rocker: documents in vivid detail a rock band's life on the road. It's a classic harkback to the days of the Crawdaddy Club, recapturing the drive and urgency that helped to make the Stones the world's greatest rock 'n' roll band. Somewhere in the melee Bobby Keys manages to pitch in with a raucous and gut-ripping tenor sax solo that spurs the whole band on to a rousing finale. (additional personnel: Bill Plummer on upright bass).

Shake Your Hips (James Moore). 2:58 mins.   Opening with stick-on-rim drumming and a guitar riff from the run-down section of town, the Stones maintain their "club days" feel on this reworked Slim Harpo song. It's a ballin' blues song straight out of the "King Bee" bag and fades out on some horny mouth-harp blowing from Michael Philip.

Casino Boogie (Jagger/Richard) 3:30 mins.   A saloon bar song making clever use of numerous two syllable word association stanzas snarled by Jagger.

Tumbling Dice (Jagger/Richard) 3:30 mins.   The Stones' current single which features Mick Taylor on bass and Jagger on guitar. Clydie King and Venetta Fields augment the vocal sound as Mick Taylor sings about love the game of chance. *[A case of muddled Micks.]*

Side Two

Sweet Virginia (Jagger/Richard) 4:25 mins.   The four cuts making up this entire side present the Stones in a semi-acoustic mood. The first track "Sweet Virginia" opens with a gently-strummed acoustic guitar and a wailing harmonica. Having set the countryesque mood another guitar picks out a secondary line prior to Mick croaking out the lyrics in a surprisingly warm voice showing no sign of strain. Deeper into the song piano (Ian Stewart), bass, drums, voices and an obligato-sax swell the sound, which finishes on a fine gutbucket sax solo.

Torn and Frayed (Jagger/Richard) 3:40 mins.   This slow lament yet again showcases the excellence of the Stones lyrics as Mick drones out the saga of the not-so-glamourous life of a rock band. The Stones don't cloak their message in obscure symbolism: they lay it straight down the line. (Additional personnel: Al Perkins, steel guitar; Jim Price Organ; Mick Taylor, bass).

Sweet Black Angel (Jagger/Richard) 3:05 mins.   A strong social statement about black militant leader Angela Davis, this is of course the flip-side of "Tumbling Dice." (Additional personnel: Amyl Nitrate, marimbas; Jimmy Miller, percussion).

Loving Cup (Jagger/Richard) 4:22 mins.   Another semi-acoustic original with piano and guitar behind the voice. This cut benefits from some strong accentuated drum work from Charlie and an instrumental backdrop of ethereal brass.

Side Three

Happy (Jagger/Richard) 3:00 mins.   Primarily a tour de force by Keith Richard who, apart from playing all the guitar and bass parts, is featured as lead singer. Coming on very strong in the "Street Fighting Man" bag, this hard fast rocker, pivots around a repeated riff highlighted by brass and interspersed by some nifty guitar licks. A standout track from Keith which poses the question for me: "Why doesn't he step into the limelight a bit more often?" (Additional personnel: Jimmy Miller, drums: Bobby Keys, percussion).

Turd on the Run (Jagger/Richard) 2:33 mins.   Another wild rocker. Keith Richard is heavily predominant, as is the piano. Jagger throws in some harp for extra good measure. (Additional personnel: Bill Plummer, upright bass).

Ventilator Blues (Jagger/Richard) 3:20 mins.   On the short-list as a possible single "Ventilator Blues" hinges around a "Spoonfull"-type whining guitar riff played over a slow and accentuated bass and drums figure. Jagger growls out the hard-hitting lyrics with menace and a hint of despair. Nice one.

I Just Want to See His Face (Jagger/Richard) 3:15 mins.   Not what you'd usually expect from Spiggy* and the lads. Virtually a hypnotic voodoo chant moaned over an ominous barrage of percussion instruments. Keith plays piano, Mick Taylor bass, and Jimmy Miller bangs a few pots 'n' pans as Clydie King, Venetta Fields and Jerry Kirkland join in the chorus.

Let It Loose (Jagger/Richard) 5:17 mins.   Typical Stones ode of unrequited love which includes a lengthy instrumental passage featuring the brass. Mick sings extremely well on this bedroom blues ballad, with a little help from Tammi Lynn, Clydie, Venetta, Dr. John, Shirley Goodman, and Joe Green.

---

* Spiggy Topes and the Turds were an all-purpose rock band invented by Peter Cook for the satirical magazine *Private Eye*. The Turds mostly satirized the Beatles and Stones, and their leader Spiggy—who deserted his wife for an avant-garde artist named OK Yoni—shared remarkably similar attitudes toward politics, art, sexual liberation, the drug laws, and birds with both John Lennon and Mick Jagger.

Side Four

All Down the Line (Jagger/Richard) 3:50 mins. Another brash rocker which roars along heightened by a great guitar break. I wouldn't be at all surprised if this was definitely pulled off the album as a follow-up single. (Additional personnel: Kathi McDonald, vocal; Bill Plummer, upright bass; Jimmy Miller, percussion).

Stop Breaking Down (Trad. Arr. Jagger/Richard/Wyman/Taylor/Watts) 3:40 mins. This is the kind of material on which the Stones really excel. A raunchy blues rocker with groin-grabbing guitars, one played by Jagger. "Old Standby" Ian Stewart is featured at the pianoforte.

Shine a Light (Jagger/Richard) 4:15 mins. Another journey through the past as the Stones re-explore their soul roots. For this track the band is helped out by the keyboard wizardry of Billy Preston, who sets the whole mood with his unmistakable sanctified licks. I'm sure this song will be well "covered"; indeed, it would make a perfect vehicle for either Aretha Franklin or Roberta Flack.

Soul Survivor (Jagger/Richard) 3:50 mins. A flag-waving closer. The Stones get down to the nitty-gritty with guitars at a premium. Builds to a thundering climax.

The Stones in L.A.: Main St. Exiles
By Robert Greenfield
Rolling Stone (San Francisco), April 27, 1972

LOS ANGELES—One year to the weekend, after the Rolling Stones played the final concert of their "farewell" tour of England, Mick Jagger is at the wheel of a big, black Mercedes, going east on Sunset Strip, Rock and Roll Billboard Row. Mick is on his way to Studio Three at Wally Heider's for another assault on a final mix for "Tumbling Dice," which will be the single from *Exile on Main Street,* the Stones' new double album, out May 7.

On June 3rd, in Seattle, Washington, it all begins again, as the Stones start their first American tour in more than two years. In six weeks, they will play some 30-odd cities.

Today, though, things are quiet, and Mick is simply on his way to work.

"Main Street" in the new album's title is in seedy, way-downtown L.A. where Mick says "You can see pimps, knives flashin', real inner city . . ." and where some of the pictures for the back cover were shot by Robert Frank, the internationally respected filmmaker and photographer. The front cover of the album is a tattoo parlour in New York City. The wall is covered with photos of strange and unusual people. Frank filmed the Stones with a Super 8 camera, then made stills out of individual frames and composed the back cover to match his original wall picture.

The album contains 18 previously unheard songs, including a Slim Harpo song written by James Moore called "Shake Your Hips," a Mick Taylor-Jagger-Richard composition "Ventilator Blues," a tune called "Happy" on which Keith Richard sings lead; the single "Tumbling Dice," and even a Jesus song: "Just Wanna See His Face."

Other titles are "Rocks Off," "All Down the Line," "Loving Cup," "Torn and Frayed," "Sweet Virginia," "Stop Breaking Down," "Sweet Black Angel," "Rip This Joint," "Shine a Light," "Turd on the Run," "Casino Boogie," "Let It Loose," and "Soul Survivor."

Most of the basic tracks were laid down almost a year ago in the basement of Keith Richard's house in the South of France. "It was cut during the summer and we'll be touring this summer so it all fits in," said Jagger. "It's a summer-y album and very commercial, I think. . . . It's a double album, like *Electric Ladyland.* God knows there was enough in that for a year's listening. . . . I expect, too, that eventually there'll be a live album coming out of the tour."

It's Saturday afternoon and sometime around the civilized hour of four or so, Mick Jagger comes padding barefoot down the stairs of his rented Bel-Air home. The house was originally owned by Marion Davies, William Randolph Hearst's protégé. The place is straight South California Gothic even now, tangles of jungle vines and underbrush by an artificial waterfall that's gone dry. The only sound around is the whisper of a sprinkler outside.

Mick sits down at the dining room table with a beer, wearing one of those shiny silk zippered jackets that sometimes have maps of Vietnam or Japan on the back. Two tigers snarl at each other across the shoulders of this one. "It's like the one we did las' time. Five cities a week for six weeks. We wanted to 'ave a rest in the middle, two weeks off to recover, but that meant we'd have been in the country more than six months and eligible for national service . . . you know, the draft."

"It'll give us a chance to play music people haven't heard us do before . . . I mean . . . . God knows I love rock and roll. Still, I'd like to see the band experiment more, with form as well as content. Because myself, I like *Satanic Majesties* . . . I mean Mick Taylor has even more strange ideas than me and I know Charlie wouldn't mind goin' along with it . . . I wouldn't wanna be a band people think they could rely on . . ."

Is it the last tour, as a band?

"Naw, I'd like ta come back and play another in the autumn meself, in all the places we missed . . . we'll be doin' a little bus tour of the deep South this time, playin' in New Orleans for the first time and in Shreveport. . . ."

"The toughest cities to find a place to play in are L.A. and San Francisco. In New York, you just do Madison Square Garden. But out here . . ." Mick reaches back and stretches . . . "one would like to do something outside, in the open air. But it's so smoggy and all. What we'll probably end up doin' is work different places around L.A., Long Beach, maybe the Palladium. In San Francisco, we'll do Winterland . . ."

Mick sighs. "But see there are problems. We'll have to do four shows at Winterland to make what we could with one at the Oakland Coliseum."

Mick, Bianca, and their baby daughter Jade have been in L.A. for four months. He's worked once, with Bobby Bland in a ballroom in Watts at three in the morning. Los Angeles has always been particularly a Stones city, the place where they come to mix and master their albums. Their music is forever coming out of car radios and jukeboxes. Nowhere else is an English accent, a velvet suit, or a ruffled shirt more in demand. Movie star tourist buses have begun to stop outside the driveway to Mick's house. "Still," he says, "the anonymity here is pretty good. It's not like England, where it's so crowded one has to buy a thousand acres, to have any privacy, where they line up outside your house to find out who you fucked the night before. I hate that place . . . you think if only they'd let you, you could take it over and really get it together because it's so small really. You think something like the miners' strike is going to really bring about a change. . . . But Heath . . ." he sighs. "Really, it's such a pathetic little village sometimes."

As for France, where he has lived since last spring, he sighs again. "Do you know there are no more salmon in the rivers of France any more?

They've killed them all with pollution. In Nice and Cannes, the French are thieves . . . I'll never live there again . . . ."

Mick goes up the stairs to gather his things. Time to go to the studio. When he comes down again he says, "People have asked me if I'm not frightened to go out on stage and work every night in America . . . maybe you shouldn't even print anything about that. . . . But, I mean, if we can't play here, in our other home so to speak, what good is it?" His voice trails away as he moves through the great dining room.

"Was this the Beach Boys' studio?" Jagger says the minute he gets inside the control room at Heider's. "I mean ai've been here before. You lose all the highs." Jimmy Miller, who's produced the Stones for years, in at the console along with Andy Johns, brother of Glyn, who is engineering tonight and in actual control of the knobs and switches. "Uh," the regular studio engineer says hesitantly, "Actually it was completely rebuilt a while ago. . . . You might still think there's too much bottom, but that's 'cause the top is going out over your head." Mick grimaces and decides to stay.

A rough mix of "Tumbling Dice" is racked up. Four guitars, two playing rhythm, one coming through a Lesley, horns, piano, organ, Mick's voice singing lead, Stones singing harmony, girls wailing background, answering the lead voice and exchanging harmonies. Dense music. "Well," Andy Johns says, after it's played through for the first time. "What do you think?"

Mick looks up at the soundproof ceiling. "I want the snares to *crack*," Mick says finally, "and the voices to *float* . . . it's tricky aw-rite. . . . You think you've got the voices susses and all of a sudden, the backing track seems so . . ." Mick stops and reaches for the word, "so . . . *ordinaire.*"

The tape is reeled and re-reeled. Andy flicks knobs and the bass recedes, the drums get crisp, the guitars overlap. "I thought you liked the cymbals like that," Andy says, after a take Mick has disapproved of. "They sound like dustbin lids," he says. Andy pouts for a second, then rewinds the tape again.

Keith Richard is lying on the roof of a big two-tone Chevy parked in front of his house, making faces at his two year-old son, Marlon, through the windshield. "Hallo," he says, climbing down, "Have you heard? They're at it again. They decided to re-mix the whole album. Been up for 31 hours so far I hear. He laughs. "Always happens. The more you mix, the better it gets."

Things are more chaotic than usual at Keith's house this day. They are packing for a four o'clock plane the next day. "We're going to Switzerland," Keith says, as Anita walks past into the kitchen looking extremely pregnant. "We figgered Marlon was lonesome, so we let it happen." Is it twins? "No," Anita says sternly, "It is the dress." She starts throwing things into what is to be the first of 19 pieces of luggage. "It was nice for me making this album," says Keith. "At the end it got a little hectic in the house what with playin' all night in the blazin' heat . . . but with the sixteen-track truck always outside and ready, we'd go downstairs whenever we felt like and work on a riff."

"I'm not even thinkin' about this tour," Keith says, concentration on coloring circles on a piece of paper with a yellow crayon he's found. "I'm just gonna show up and be on it. I wish we'd work some places we haven't been through, like Kansas City. We've only been to Memphis once . . . y'get hung up in the same old circuit of cities all the time. . . . We've got a short list of people we'd like to take with us, the Staple Singers, Joe Tex . . . an old bluesman would be nice but they're pretty fragile . . ."

"By the time we get 'round to doin' it, it'll be almost as long a gap as between the last and the one before it. Funny though how things have changed, no one's talkin' about free concerts anymore and yet right now grass is legal in Michigan. It's like maybe when you stop pushin', you get what you want . . . there's a message there somewhere folks. . . ."

Will it be the last tour?

Keith looks up from his coloring. "I doubt it," he says. "We need the money." Keith's worked only once since he's been in L.A., an attempted jam with Chuck Berry. Mr B. kept casting nervous glances at Mick, who was attracting all the attention at one side of the stage, then asked Keith to "turn down." Finally he asked him and the piano player, Mac Rebbenack, Dr. John, to leave. Now, Keith puts some of the dubs from their new album on the record player. "I wanted to release 'Sweet Virginia' as kind of an easy listening single," he says. The refrain in that song is "Scrape the shit right off your shoes."

Keith says the Stones might work a festival in the English countryside this summer. They've learned it's legal for them to work there: "Either

that or Lebanon." There's a short silence. A festival in Lebanon? "Yeah," Keith says, matter-of-fact. "Might be a gas, actually."

The phone rings and Keith picks it up. "They've got the new mixes at Marshall's house," he says, "Let's go."

Things are slightly crazy in Marshall Chess' little pool house over-looking the lights of Hollywood. Chris O'Dell, the Stones do-everything lady in L.A., is on the phone looking for a piano player. Mick might want to cut a promotional jingle for radio about the album. "Billy Preston isn't home," she explains earnestly. "Stevie Wonder's available but I haven't asked Mick about him. . . . I called Carole King and she said, well, she wasn't work-ing much anymore, what with the baby and all."

Jimmy Miller comes through the door with his hands full of album sleeves. "Take that shit off," he says, "and play something good. We've re-done five songs."

All the mixes of "Tumbling Dice" are played, loud and numbing. Marshall's on the phone making arrangements so he can hand-carry the masters onto the plane and deliver them to Atlantic Records in person on Monday morning.

THE REVIEWS

With the sun fading behind the hills and the light failing, Mick and Keith sit slumped on the couch. In the gathering gloom, all you can see is their wan white faces and feathered hair. They look like brothers.

The last chords of "Tumbling Dice" fade away. "They're both good, y'know Jimmy," Mick says, closing his eyes. "Maybe the old one . . . ," Keith mumbled. Jimmy looks around. He says, "I think the new one is more commercial." The two are almost identical; even Mick can't tell the difference. They discuss it around the room. The old one, the new one. Which one will sound better mono? The old one. "OK," Jimmy concedes, "the old one, We'll go back now and play with it." "Yeah," Andy Johns agrees, "just a fraction more top on it. It's still a bit dull."

Across the room, Marshall Chess is talking to himself. Jimmy and Andy collect the mixes. Mick Jagger grabs a piece of paper and draws the album title the way he wants it. "Fanatics," Marshall says to himself, softly. He sputters a laugh, "Fanatics."

The new Rolling Stones album is ready to be delivered.

BIBLIOGRAPHY

Aeppeli, Felix. *The Rolling Stones Ultimate Guide.* Bromley, U.K.: R.I.S., 1996.

Aftel, Mandy. *Death of a Rolling Stone: The Brian Jones Story.* London: Sidgwick and Jackson, 1983.

Bockris, Victor. *Keith Richards.* London: Hutchinson, 1992.

Bonanno, Massimo. *The Rolling Stones Chronicles.* London: Plexus, 1990.

Booth, Stanley. *The True Adventures of the Rolling Stones.* London: Heinemann, 1985.

———. *Keith: Standing in the Shadows.* New York: St. Martins Press, 1995.

Burroughs, William. *The Naked Lunch.* London: John Calder, 1964.

Carr, Roy. *The Rolling Stones Illustrated.* London: N.E.L., 1976.

Christgau, Robert. *Rock Albums of the 70s.* London: Vermillion, 1982.

Dent, Dr. John Yerbury. *Anxiety and Its Treatment.* London: Skeffington, 1955.

Fong-Torres, Ben. *Hickory Wind.* New York: Simon and Schuster, 1991.

Greenfield, Robert. *STP—Stones Touring Party.* London: Michael Joseph, 1974.

Hotchner, A. E. *Blown Away.* London: Simon and Schuster, 1990.

Karnbach, James, and Carol Bernson. *Complete Recording Guide to the Rolling Stones.* London: Aurum Press, 1997.

Melly, George. *Revolt into Style.* Harmondsworth: Penguin, 1970.

Norman, Phillip. *The Stones.* London: Hamish Hamilton, 1984.

Rawlings, T., K. Badman, and A. Neill. *Good Times Bad Times.* Complete Music. London, 1997.

Rebennack, M. (Dr. John). *Under a Hoodoo Moon.* New York: St. Martins Press, 1994.

Sanchez, Spanish Tony. *Ups and Downs with the Rolling Stones.* Glebe, N.S.W., Australia: Wild and Woolley, 1979.

Wyman, Bill. *Stone Alone.* London: Viking, 1990.

Zollo, Paul. *Songwriters on Songwriting.* Da Capo: New York, 1997.

Film and TV

BBC TV. *Old Grey Whistle Test.* Montreux rehearsals for U.S. tour, May 1972. "If Keith won't come to rehearsals, rehearsals must come to Keith."

BBC TV. *Old Grey Whistle Test.* October 1974. Keith Richards interview. "World's Most Gratuitously Stoned Human Being, The."

Collectors' uncut footage. *New Musical Express* Poll Winners Concert, 1965. Annual spring celebration of *NME* readers' favorite groups playing Wembley Pool. The broadcast footage is widely exchanged among collectors. "Raw," unedited footage is also in very limited circulation.

Frank, Robert, dir. *Cocksucker Blues.* Not on general release.

Lindsay-Hogg, Michael, dir. *The Rolling Stones Rock 'n' Roll Circus* (1968). 1996 Abkco.

Maysles, Albert and David, dir. *Gimme Shelter,* 1970.

Pallenberg, Anita, and Keith Richards. Home movies.

Ready Steady Go! London's hippest weekly television program—practically the Stones' private fiefdom between 1964 and 1966. The weekend starts here! Such footage as survives is owned by the gifted English drummer Dave Clark, whose company has issued segments of various shows on videocassette. Authentic footage is intercut with film of the Dave Clark Five, in a manner that could lead the credulous to believe the Dave Clark Five appeared on *Ready Steady Go!*

Roeg, Nicolas, and Donald Cammell. *Performance* (1968). 1970 Warner Bros.

Whitehead, Peter, dir. *Charlie Is My Darling.* Not on general release.

ACKNOWLEDGMENTS

The author and the publisher are grateful for permission to quote from the following:

Review of *Exile on Main St.* by Richard Williams, from *Melody Maker,* May 1972. Copyright © Richard Williams/*Melody Maker.*/IPC Magazines Ltd. Used by permission.

Review of *Exile on Main St.* by Lenny Kaye, from *Rolling Stone,* July 1972. Copyright © Straight Arrow Publishers, Inc. Used by permission.

The Stones in L.A: Main St. Exiles by Robert Greenfield, from *Rolling Stone,* April 1972. Copyright © Straight Arrow Publishers, Inc. Used by permission.

Review of *Exile on Main St.* by Don Heckman, from *The New York Times,* June 4, 1972. Copyright © *The New York Times.* Used by permission.

Review of *Exile on Main St.* by Roy Carr, from *New Musical Express,* April 1972. Copyright © Roy Carr/NME/IPC Magazines Ltd. Used by permission.

Interview: "Anita Pallenberg—Homes and Gardens" by John Perry. Copyright © 1999 Pallenberg/Perry. Used by permission.

INDEX

Page references to photos are printed in italics.